GOD IN THE MACHINE

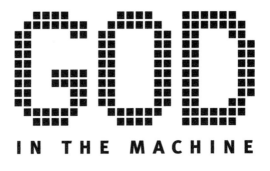

IN THE MACHINE

Video Games as Spiritual Pursuit

Liel Leibovitz

TEMPLETON PRESS

Templeton Press
300 Conshohocken State Road, Suite 500
West Conshohocken, PA 19428
www.templetonpress.org

Designed and typeset by Gopa & Ted2, Inc.

ISBN 978-1-59947-437-3

Library of Congress Cataloging-in-Publication
Data on file

Printed in the United States of America

13 14 15 16 17 18   10 9 8 7 6 5 4 3 2 1

An Invocation

Mariners sailing close to the shores of Tuscany heard
a voice call out from the hills, the trees, and the sky.
The great god Pan is dead. Pan, god of Panic. The sudden
awareness that everything is alive and significant. The date
was December 25, 1 AD. But Pan lives on in the realm
of imagination. In writing, painting, and music. Look at
van Gogh's Sunflowers, writhing with pretentious life.
Listen to the Pipes of Pan in Jajouka. Now Pan is
neutralized, framed in museums, entombed in books,
and relegated to folklore. But art is spilling out of its frames
into subway graffiti. Will it stop there? Consider an
apocalyptic statement: nothing is true everything is
permitted; Hasaan I Sabah, the old man in the mountain.
Not to be interpreted as an invitation to all manner
of unrestrained and destructive behavior, that would
be a minor episode, which would run its course. Everything
is permitted because nothing is true. It is all make-believe . . .
illusion . . . dream . . . art. When art leaves the frame and
the written word leaves the page, not merely the physical frame
and page, but the frames and pages that assign the categories.
A basic disruption of reality itself occurs. The literal realization
of art. Success will write apocalypse across the sky.[1]

WILLIAM S. BURROUGHS, "APOCALYPSE."

Contents

Introduction

Every time anyone asks me what I do for a living, I take a moment to cherish the answer: I'm a video game scholar. The pleasure of hearing myself say these words never subsides; I imagine seven-year-old me, delighted with the report from the future informing him that he'll soon figure out a way to continue to play games uninterrupted while convincing the rest of adult society that his is a worthwhile pursuit. But no sooner do I give my answer than a torrent of other questions is unleashed: Aren't video games a waste of time? Don't they cause violence? Aren't they overly misogynistic, outrageously homophobic, irredeemably imperialist? Might it not be said that they're too simplistic to tell complicated stories? Don't they dull the mind? Aren't they incurably addictive? Is it not true that they're the favorite pastime of school shooters, lone gunmen, and other maniacs? Are they not just a fad? Are they not just for kids? Are they not, in a word, bad?

These are all serious questions, and they've received their fair share of attempted answers. For nearly two decades now, game scholars, a rapidly growing group, has been conducting psychological experiments, tracking eye movements and heart rates, analyzing plot progressions, interviewing gamers and developers and parents, and applying a wide array of methodologies to provide a better understanding of just what games are and just why so many people play them for such extended periods of time. If you've contemplated any of the aforementioned questions seriously, you may be relieved that the answer to all of them, simply put, is no. But that is hardly an illumination: with nearly two decades of study, what we've achieved is mainly a solid collection of insights into all of the things that games *are not*. What we still lack is a convincing argument concerning what they *are*.

This question is neither abstract nor trivial. Observing the young at play, parents and educators are justified for feeling puzzled when they see that singularly focused look on their loved ones' faces, notice the rapid twitching of thumbs, hear the cacophony of explosions and howls and shrieks, and are struck by the rapid pace at which things unfurl, a rhythm much too fast to allow rational thought any time to do its contemplative work. They may also be forgiven for wondering not only about the benefits of gaming but also about its joys—what, after all, is the satisfaction of furiously pressing all these buttons without pause or reprieve? And what may be the pleasures of characters who seem so one-dimensional, pixilated psychopaths with nothing but digital carnage on their mind?

Such quizzical observations are not to be taken lightly. In fact, they are the point of departure from which this book launches its investigation. And an investigation it is, offering meditations rather than pronouncements, embracing uncertainties, and seeking—as a poet who would have likely made a very enthusiastic gamer once put it—the "still point of the turning world." That still point turns out to be one that is wholly unexpected: as I endeavor to show in this brief book, the human construct with which video games have most in common isn't television or literature or warfare but religion. Playing games calls on the same faculties as does shuffling into shul early on Friday afternoon or rising to church on a Sunday morning. It is a practice in rituals, ethics, morality, and metaphysics. And while such a claim lies beyond the realm of the empirically measurable, there may very well be a good case that playing video games makes one, if not a more moral person, then at the very least a person more acutely attuned to morality's subtle impositions. And the reason may very well be that video games, their bad reputation be damned, are a godly medium.

This claim may sound audacious. It is not. Consider the evidence. As it sets out to order the world, religion must first face a host of questions pertaining to the relations between the world's creator or creators and the creation, us meek mortals. Religion must explain just what that said creator demands, and decide whether it believes we have the right to refuse. And religion does so, generally, by presenting us with a foundational story and a set of fundamental rules. The story explains the origins of the universe to us, its believers, and then dictates a list of expected behaviors: Don't eat pork. Take Communion. Pray five times a day. Hurt no living creature. Recite these texts each day, each week, each year. As further motivation, religion offers a set of rewards for compliance, as well as various punishments for different magnitudes of transgression. And religion is sufficiently layered so as to welcome into its fold a host of believers, each willing to accept some but rarely all of its strictures. Religion, then, is exacting but modular, rule-based but tolerant of deviation, moved by metaphysical yearnings but governed by intricate, earthly designs. Religion is a game.

Which is in no way belittling religion—I will soon show precisely these playful elements have made religion so prevalent, and precisely the religious undertones that have made games so indispensable to the evolution of culture. Rather than think about them as disparate entities, one sacred and the other profane, it is time to consider them together, two pursuits that share practices and sensibilities, two ways of contemplating urgent questions that defy reason and turn to faith instead.

There are, of course, important differences between games and religion. Game designers are not gods. Games are not the world. The comparison only extends so far. But as video games continue their cultural ascent, and as so many of us continue to cling to our misconceptions, we would do well to pursue new ways of thinking, even wild and imperfect ones, if we are ever to make sense of what is rapidly becoming our era's defining medium. If we do, we may discover that what so many of us perceived as a terrible new imposition is neither new nor terrible, but rather an oddly premodern way of being in the world that is deeply interested in questions of right and wrong, being and nothingness, and all the other conundrums that have had us scratching our heads for millennia. Everything that follows should be taken in this spirit.

God in the Machine

Thinking inside the Box

GAME DESIGN, GLORY, AND THE SEARCH FOR GOD

In March 2013 the Museum of Modern Art in Manhattan debuted a new exhibit, titled *Applied Design*, featuring the newest acquisitions to MoMA's permanent collection: fourteen classic video games, including *Pac-Man*, *Tetris*, and *The Sims*.[1] That the same hallowed halls reserved for Picasso now also displayed Pac-Man sparked yet another round of a now familiar debate: Are video games art?

Whatever the answer, whatever the position, the debate revolved around the same set of ethereal arguments that are called to earth whenever art is being discussed. Supporters of MoMA's canonization of digital entertainment pointed out that video games, like all great art, expand our horizons; opponents argued that lacking a single creator, and being primarily playthings, video games fall short of pure art's Olympian standards.

It's a fascinating debate, but the answer to the above question is, put bluntly, "no." Video games aren't art because they are, quite thoroughly, something else: code.

To understand the distinction, consider *Pac-Man*, which was at the heart of one of the most important—and most unheralded—lawsuits in the history of the medium. In 1982, with the *Pac-Man* craze peaking, an aspiring company named Artic International released its own series of video arcade games featuring more or less the same maze, the same pastel-hued ghosts, and the same ravenous big-mouthed circle. The color pattern was slightly different than the original, and the game's name was tweaked—it was called *Puckman*—but it was clearly a knockoff. Midway, *Pac-Man*'s American manufacturer and distributor, sued.

Artic's defense was artful. According to Title 17 of the U.S. Code, Artic argued, copyright protection applied to "original works of authorship fixed in any tangible medium of expression." Unlike a page, which is a repository for printed words, or a film strip, which permanently stores images, the computer chips that made *Pac-Man* run held nothing fixed; like all code, they were merely a set of instructions that, when followed, allowed the machine to conjure the famous character and his world. As such, Artic argued, video games did not meet the requirement for fixation. The company even cited a congressional report from the mid-1970s, arguing that "the definition of 'fixation' would exclude from the concept purely evanescent or transient reproductions, such as those . . . captured momentarily in the 'memory' of a computer." The judge, however, was unconvinced. Video games, he ruled, may be a set of instructions, but they're a very consistent set of instructions; *Pac-Man* looked exactly the same every time the machine was turned on. Artic was forced to cease production and pay damages.

Puckman lost the battle, but it ended up winning the war. Immediately after the case was decided, the U.S. Copyright Office announced that it was changing its approach to video games. Rather than allow game producers to register the images and sounds that appear on the screen as "audiovisual work" and the code itself as "literary work," they would now require applicants to choose between the two.

Most game producers chose to protect the way their games looked and sounded and felt, their iconic characters and memorable landscapes. This is unsurprising. We love Mario and Link and Master Chief, not the algorithms that govern their movements. But there's more to this strategy: game producers quickly realized that, unlike art, which is distinct and unique and exists for its own aesthetic purposes, code is practical and interchangeable and exists merely as a tool to make something work. Trying to copyright code, then, was a lot like trying to copyright a hammer—even if you succeeded in protecting one particular design, other people could still construct very similar methods of banging nails into walls.

With code largely unprotected, designers are not above the occasional bout of copying and pasting. Take a look, for example, at *Crush the Castle*, originally released in April 2009. You probably haven't heard of it, but you've almost certainly seen or played a nearly identical game that came out eight months later, used the same general premise—catapulting objects onto stacked structures—but replaced the warring knights with angry birds.

This isn't theft. It's how games work. Even though they were algorithmic twins, the two games couldn't have felt any more different: one was cool and steely and evoked the raw conflict of medieval times, and the other had those villainous green pigs and enough charm to become instantly iconic.

Which brings us back to the argument about video games as art. You could argue that *Angry Birds* succeeded where *Crush the Castle* fizzled because the former was more artfully done. But that would be only half true, as the game itself—specifically the playing experience, of swiping fingers to flick objects across the screen—is, for all intents and purposes, the same game. With art, borrowing and citing and paraphrasing images and themes and ideas is commonplace; it's how the craft is practiced. But a game incorporating another game's code isn't like Duchamp incorporating the *Mona Lisa* in his work. That's because a few lines of code aren't an artistic statement but rather an action-oriented script that performs a specific set of functions, and computers know how to do only so many functions. While art is bound only by its creator's imagination, code is bound by the limitations, more numerous than you'd imagine, of computer comprehension. Code can't, like Joyce's *Finnegan's Wake*, abandon logic and decide to imitate the sounds of nature instead. It can never be poetry, just a series of if/then statements. Code has more in common with the hinges that connect the museum's doors to their frames than it does with *Nude Descending a Staircase*.

This divide between code and image, between the algorithms responsible for the experience of play and the pixels representing its visual manifestation, is what makes games so complicated and compelling. MoMA, however, has chosen to largely ignore this question; a number of the games displayed in its exhibition are merely loops of video footage, allowing visitors to watch, as the museum put it, "guided tours of these alternate worlds," but not to play the games themselves.

The question, then, is not whether video games are art, but whether whatever is currently gracing MoMA's walls could even be called video games. Anyone who has ever been truly transformed by a game—that is, anyone who realizes that games, unlike paintings or movies or books, are made not to be observed but to be actively played, repeatedly and over long stretches of time—knows that the answer is no.

What, then, are they? If we find them worthy of eternal life in our museums, this question is pressing. The Dutch theorist Johan Huizinga provided an answer in his seminal study, *Homo Ludens*, which pertains to all forms of play. While many human undertakings, he argued, are structured similarly to play—trials have rules, wars have winners and losers—play is predicated on three overarching requirements: it must be voluntary, it must follow its own scripted logic, and it must stand apart in space and time from all other activities. Often, Huizinga's ideas are compressed even further and represented by his one key concept, that of the magic circle: to play, he wrote, is to bring perfection into an imperfect world, muting, for a short while, all of life's uncertainties and insisting instead on far simpler sequences. Think of yourself, at seven or eight, playing hide-and-seek: your eyes closed, you count to a hundred, and when you open them again the world has been reduced to a singular and comprehensible task. For a spell, life is about nothing more than looking behind trees or under the bed, trying to find your friends, your pulse quickening with each discovery.

But such sublime simplicity doesn't occur naturally. It depends on rules. Hide-and-seek appeals so greatly because its rules are so simple: we know how long we must count, where we may and may not hide, and how much time the seeker is allotted before the remaining players are permitted to pop out of their hiding spots and declare victory. When we disagree about the rules, contention ensues and the magic circle breaks. We are reminded that we are still in and of the world, and reminded, too, of all of the world's ambiguities and complexities. For play to sustain itself and thrive, then, the rules must be clear.

That, of course, is not too tall an order when all players are human; a few quibbles and quarrels later, most of us, when contemplating even the most complicated play settings, are likely to agree on a basic premise. But when play depends on the interaction between a human being and a machine, things grow endlessly more complicated. Machines have no use for magic circles. They make no distinction between their motivations. They have no motivations. They run series of algorithms, producing calculations. When it comes to playing, they're terrible, unimaginative bores. To bring down Joshua, the renegade computer on the brink of launching a nuclear war with the Soviet Union in the 1983 classic *War Games*, the boyish and brilliant hacker, Matthew Broderick, instructs the machine to play tic-tac-toe against itself. Joshua, frustrated by the inevitable string of draws, learns the concept of futility, which so overwhelms him—even supercomputers cringe when faced with philosophical abstractions—that he decides to stop playing. How are video game designers, then, to avoid the Joshua trap? How are they to devise a series of encounters between human beings and algorithms that would not reduce us to a heap of calculations or send our machines into fits of existential despair, unable to comprehend our complex emotional concepts?

These core questions at the heart of game design are staggeringly complex. Addressing them, game scholars sometimes argue that video games are a triumphant medium precisely because they've solved these conundrums, and the solution has to do with interactivity. Our technologies, goes the argument, have become so advanced that they now allow for a real dialogue between us and our computers. We have no more Joshuas, obdurate golems that must be subdued. Our machines are smart now. They have, to use a favorite buzzword of the era, artificial intelligence. They're capable of learning, and we've become adept at teaching them. And video games are at the fore of this revolution, because they allow us to engage harmoniously with machines not in some workaday production process but in the transcendent realm of play.

It's a very compelling theory. It's also completely false.

Of all the fallacies marring our understanding of video games, none, perhaps, is more vexing than the idea that video games represent the next evolutionary stage of technology because, unlike its anemic ancestors, it fosters a sort of conversation, however primitive, between humans and machine. Video games cannot do that, at least not yet. But understanding our desire for this sort of interaction is key, as we currently celebrate video games more for what they cannot do than for what they can.

What they cannot do is *interact*. The term is tricky: without being too persnickety, we must first understand what we mean by "interaction," a term too nebulous to do us any real good. For a solid beginning, we may turn to the old sociologists, like Ervin Goffman, who remind us that we all, being human, coexist in a social sphere and depend on a modicum of exchange or interplay with our fellow humans, an interplay guided by a specific set of rules, norms, myths, and symbols.[2] Pursue this logic and you're likely to emerge with strong ideas about what the ideal interaction might be: two or more people, meeting face to face, unobtrusively observing each other's expressions, movements, and intonations. Our language, too, has internalized this bias: when we agree with someone, we see eye to eye, and when we express faith in another we take that person at face value. Physical proximity indicates an accord, a harmonious joining together of two bodies and two souls.

What, then, are machines to do? Most theorists suppose that they, poor eyeless and faceless and soulless automatons, should strive to imitate us humans, or, at least, aspire to engage us as much as possible. A perfect communications medium, wrote one observer, is therefore one in which "the sender and receiver use all their senses, the reply is immediate, the communication is usually close circuit, and the content is primarily informal,"[3] not too far a cry from two friends greeting each other in the street. A similar approach prevails even when the medium in question does something other than connect two human beings across space and time. Fantasizing on the possibilities of interactive life in *Newsweek* magazine in the early 1990s, for example, one writer imagined:

> a huge amount of information available to anyone at the touch of a button, everything from airline sched-ules to esoteric scientific journals to video versions of off-off-off Broadway. Watching a movie won't be a passive experience. At various points, you'll click on alternative story lines and create your individualized version of "Terminator XII." Consumers will send as well as receive all kinds of data. . . . Video-camera own-ers could record news they see and put it on the uni-versal network. . . . Viewers could select whatever they

> wanted just by pushing a button. . . . Instead of playing
> rented tapes on their VCRs, . . . [the customers] may
> be able to call up a movie from a library of thousands
> through a menu displayed on the TV. Game fanatics
> may be able to do the same from another electronic
> library filled with realistic video versions of arcade
> shoot-'em-ups. . . .[4]

The paragraph's predictions are prescient, but their accuracy is hardly the issue: interactive technologies excite us because they carry a promise that transcends mere utility, the promise of communion with powers greater and unknown. Writing in the ninth century and reversing centuries of contempt for technical know-how as the domain of uneducated laborers, the philosopher Johannes Scotus Eriugena noted that the useful arts represented "man's links with the Divine, their cultivation a means to salvation."[5] Media scholar Colin Cherry was channeling Eriugena when he claimed, somewhat more mutely, that any new technology must be measured based on whether it "has offered people new liberties of action."[6]

But what might these liberties be? What new freedoms are on offer? Three decades or more after first inquiring into the nature of interactivity, we are left primarily with complications. "The common feeling," one observer summed it up neatly, "is that interactivity, like news, is something you know when you see it."[7] Thinkers who have tried to be a touch more specific often failed to come up with anything drastically more instructive. "Part and parcel of a system is the notion of 'relationship.' . . . Interactional systems then, shall be two or more communicants in the process of, or at the level of, defining the nature of their relationship,"[8] argued one thinker, while another claimed that "something is interactive when people can participate as agents within a representational context. (An agent is 'one who initiates actions.')"[9] Taking a literal approach, one media scholar defined "interactivity" as "the ability to intervene in a meaningful way *within the representation itself,* not to *read* it differently. Thus interactivity in music would mean the ability to change the sound, interactivity in painting to change colors, or make marks, interactivity in film . . . the ability to change the way the movie comes out."[10] For another, it meant "a cyclical process in which two actors alternately listen, think, and speak. The quality of interaction depends on the quality of each of the subtasks (listening, thinking, and speaking)."[11]

Such definitions can be intermittently instructive, but they offer little insight into the inherent nature of video games. Video games do something very different, which game design scholars Katie Salen and Eric Zimmerman captured neatly in their seminal book on the subject, *Rules of Play*. "Game designers," they wrote, "do not directly design play. They only design the structures and contexts in which play takes place, indirectly shaping the actions of the players. We call the space of future action implied by a game design the *space of possibility*. It is the space of all possible actions that might take place in a game, the space of all possible meanings which can emerge from a game design."[12]

Video games, then, are not, as far as our traditional definitions apply, interactive media. They do not talk back to the user. They do not allow a person and a machine to take turns as sender and receiver of information, at least not in any meaningful way. Instead, they offer players a limited number of choices: go left or right, swing the sword or jump, fight one enemy or another. This is a far cry from the sort of interaction we dream about when we dream of a world perfected by machines; instead of opening up new liberties and infinite interpretations, video games redefine interaction by placing us in a carefully designed environment that permits us the freedom to do little more than merely negotiate the limited number of alternatives on offer.

Just how limited these alternatives truly are is surprising. Play tic-tac-toe, for example, and the game's simple rules—a nine-slot grid, two players, the goal being placing one's mark in three horizontal, vertical, or diagonal slots while blocking the opponent from doing the same—open up, if we allow for symmetry, 255,168 distinct possibilities. Perhaps for that reason, the game was featured so prominently in *War Games*: it lulls players into a false sense of simplicity, revealing its immense number of possibilities only when play is in full swing. Like nearly all games, tic-tac-toe is what theorist Jepser Juul calls a *game of emergence*, which is to say a game that sets forth a small number of simple rules from which a vast number of scenarios could unfurl, with the rules themselves, and nothing but them, constituting the framework of the game. Think of baseball or skipping rope or playing catch: these demand a set of rules specific enough to guarantee an orderly progression of play yet fluid enough to permit individual innovation. When we watch such a game take place, we often assign it additional layers of meaning, some superimposed narrative to help us make sense of the proceedings. Few and rare are those of us who can turn on a televised ballgame, say, and not immediately gravitate toward one team or another; Dwight D. Eisenhower had it just right when he quipped that an atheist was someone who watched Notre Dame play SMU and didn't care who won.

Video games, on the other hand, are much simpler creatures, and they belong, all by themselves, to the group Juul called *games of progression*, in which the strict logic of algorithms governs all. Differences between the two categories abound. We watch a basketball game, say, in part for the slim possibility that a player will lose his cool, say, leap to the stands, and attempt to throttle a heckling spectator; such moments are uncommon, but they tend to lodge themselves in our collective memory because they reaffirm that oldest of clichés: anything can happen. When we play a video game, on the other hand, the only things that can happen are those prescribed by the designer and etched into the game's code.

There is no room for chance or deviation: every time we press the button, the little pixilated character on the screen jumps exactly as high as it had the time before. If tic-tac-toe, then, presents us with more than a quarter of a million distinct scenarios, video games often present us with just one. Look at Nintendo's original *Legend of Zelda*, for example, and you're likely to see a simple flow-chart: the game is nothing but a series of puzzles, each with only one correct solution, each necessary in order to advance. To win, the player must simply go through the motions, from dungeon to dungeon and from riddle to riddle, with no choice but to follow the designer's narrow path.

This, at least, is what games feel like when they are poorly designed. Take, for example, the following review of the game *Eragon*, which appeared on Gamespot, one of the most popular and influential game review websites:

> Certain objects in the environment can be moved or rearranged using your magic. It's not very interesting, though, because you can't choose what you interact with or how you do it. Instead, it's usually along the lines of moving a pile of conveniently placed loose boards to create a makeshift bridge between two platforms.[13]

Or the review of the first-person-shooter, *World War II Combat: Iwo Jima*:

> The objectives are all laid out right in front of you, so at least you don't have to go searching all over a level to find what you're looking for. In fact, the game actively discourages you from wandering off the beaten path by placing invisible mines all along the pathway, so if you try to go exploring, you'll get blown sky high. All of the enemies you fight look identical, and they all act

like idiots. Some enemies will run right up to you and start firing wildly, sometimes expending full clips from point-blank range without hitting you once. Sometimes the enemies will just stand there and fire their rifles straight up into the air, which is rather bizarre. What's more bizarre is that they'll often hit you even though their guns aren't aimed in your direction. Even more annoying is that the same random fire works both ways. Sometimes when you have a dead aim on an enemy's head, you can blast away and get no response. Other times you can use the sniper rifle for a one-hit kill with a well-placed footshot.[14]

The problem with both games has nothing to do with realism, artistry, or even a failure to obey the basic rules of physics. The problem is that both failed to construct a closed and sensible system, a system that posited clearly defined rules that made sense within its own confines and that allowed the player to explore its carefully constructed worlds on the player's own terms. Call attention to the fact that only certain, predetermined objects are movable, or that exploration is limited to narrow paths alone, and you commit the gravest sin of video games: reminding players that they're nothing but pawns in a hermetically sealed universe crafted by an unknown creator, playing by rules they will never entirely understand.

To avoid subjecting their players to such a state of existential ennui, game designers came up with principles intended to safeguard the purity of the play experience—three principles in particular. As design scholar Doug Church put it in a seminal 1999 article, games must allow players to create a sense of intention, present perceivable consequences, and immerse themselves in the narrative.[15] The first principle is the most crucial. Intention means allowing the player to make an implementable plan of the player's own creation, a plan influenced by a reading of the game's possible options. The opening scene of 2012's *Assassin's Creed III*, the most recent installment in the popular series, provides a fine example of the intention principle at play. The protagonist, an assassin named Haytham, must stab one of his nemeses as the latter is enjoying a play from the comfort of his own box at the theater. Exploring his surroundings, Haytham soon discovers a ladder and climbs up to the rafters. The player is free to weigh all possible options: Might Haytham leap down onto the stage and sprint across it, dagger at hand? Try that, and you'll get caught by guards. What about an alternate path to the enemy's lair? Go ahead and look; one doesn't exist. It takes the novice player a minute or two, and perhaps several ill-advised attempts at a solution, to realize that a giant cardboard sun, part of the play's scenery, is hanging nearby, and that Haytham can easily use it as a stepping-stone en route to his destination. The move, of course, is the only one available to the player; there's no other way to complete that particular challenge. But it's presented in a way that allows the player to take note, analyze, plan, and implement. When the player finally presses the right button and executes the right move, the outcome feels entirely deserved, the fruit of one's own labors: "It was me," the player mumbles, satisfied. "I made this happen."

Intention works in this fashion, but it isn't enough. To guide the player through the game's world, each action taken must have a perceivable consequence, a greater challenge than it seems: in the early days of gaming, for example, when computational power was insufficient, game designers focused only on the few objects necessary to the progression of the plot, leaving gamers frustrated and confused: Why, for example, did nothing happen when they shot at any door in a given maze except for the one that led to the next level? Did that door have magical properties? That made no sense, and it not only pulled the player out of the game—calling attention to its artifice—but also made for a poor play experience.

With the conditions of the game's world set seemingly at random, players had little to go on as they attempted to observe patterns and plan their course.

To present the game's perceivable consequences clearly, and to allow for the creation of intention, games must tell good stories. Video game narratives, however, are a species apart, one that has little in common with the storytelling craft that other platforms have perfected. For the first two decades of the medium's existence, scholars and critics alike, assuming that video games were in essence nothing more than television with a few interactive elements thrown in sporadically and for good measure, paid close attention to the question of narrative, insisting that video games tell stories in more or less the same ways that films or television shows did. Instead, as MoMA's misguided act of curation teaches us, video games tell stories through action. They are only marginally concerned with traditional narratives: plot lines and characters, of course, are on display, but they are largely inconsequential to the player's experience. A host of tentative experiments I've conducted demonstrates that well. In one, I asked a host of self-proclaimed gaming enthusiasts to recall a movie they had seen and a video game they had played in the last three weeks and describe the plots of both in as much detail as they could muster. Almost without exception, respondents recalled much of the films' plots, including characters' names, secondary or tertiary story lines, and small, detailed flourishes. Things were very different when it came to describing games: here, character names were mentioned only infrequently, major plot points were glossed over or altogether ignored, and undue attention was often paid to extremely minor points in the game that just happened to be the most recent challenge to frustrate or intrigue the individual gamer. The result was a stack of descriptions so cryptic that follow-up interviews were often required to identify the games in question.

These results, of course, are far from conclusive, but they shouldn't surprise anyone who has ever taken a game controller to hand. As I explore in greater detail in the next chapter, the play experience is far from a detached, subjective, rational experience. It is, in addition to being considerably more physical than commonly assumed, a series of rapid and intertwined decisions.

Jesper Juul, then, was right on target when he suggested that we think of a video game as a state machine: "A game is actually what computer science describes as a state machine. It is a system that can be in different states. It contains input and output functions, as well as definitions of what state and what input will lead to what following state. When you play a game, you are interacting with the state machine that is the game. In a board game, this state is stored in the position of the pieces on the board, in computer games the state is stored as variables, and then represented on the screen."[16] To ensure that Juul's state machine runs smoothly, designers have devised several models, often formed as questions a designer must consider at each stage of the game's progression. Salen and Zimmerman summed them up in their model of an anatomy of choice, differentiating between internal events, which are part of the game's hidden architecture, and external events, which are clearly visible to the player:[17]

> What happened before the player was given the choice? (internal event)
> How is the possibility of choice conveyed to the player? (external event)
> How did the player make the choice? (internal event)
> What is the result of the choice? How will it affect future choices? (internal event)
> How is the result of the choice conveyed to the player? (external event)

Meeting these conditions, however, is not always an easy task. In *Trigger Happy*,[18] his meditation on video games, writer Steven Poole, thinking along similar lines as Salen and Zimmerman, defined three mistakes—or "incoherencies"—that game designers often repeat, which he labeled as incoherencies of causality, function, and space. The first incoherency occurs when similar actions have different consequences, depending on the convenience of the narrative arc. If, for example, as is the case in many poorly designed games, a player can eradicate enemies using an atomic laser cannon, yet that very same omnipotent weapon has little or no effect on a wooden door—which can only be opened with a key hidden somewhere in the game—a causal incoherence occurs. Similarly, functional incoherencies occur when objects obtained throughout the course of game play may be used in certain contexts but not others. A wind-generating boomerang in *The Legend of Zelda: Twilight Princess*, for example, is capable of transporting bombs across the screen in some fight sequences yet fails to do so in others. The player, having a rational expectation that actions will have similar consequences every time they are repeated, is likely to be baffled by such inconsistencies. Finally, spatial incoherencies occur when certain actions are appropriate in some spaces but not in other, similar ones. Again, *Zelda* provides an excellent example. At some points in the game, Link, the protagonist, is transformed into a wolf. In his lupine form, he is able to dig underneath obstacles such as fences or walls, but not all fences or walls: when lupine Link attempts to dig in a space that was not specifically designated by the designers as requiring digging, nothing happens. If identical spaces require different actions, the player has no way of making, to borrow Church's useful term, "an implementable plan."

At the core of video game storytelling, then, is not a linear and rational and passive progression of events but a set of available actions. To be coherent, to be compelling, video games must unfold in a way that allows players to continue and believe that the decisions they make are their own, and that the game's world, preordained as it is, nonetheless allows for expressions of their free will. Video games, in other words, depend much on the sentiment expressed by the Jewish sage Rabbi Akiva, in *Pirkei Avot*: "Everything is foreseen, and permission is granted."

The theological language is not unmerited; in fact, it captures much of what is at the very core of the gaming experience. Huizinga was thinking along these lines when he wrote, "For Archaic man, doing and daring are power, but knowing is magical power. For him all particular knowledge is sacred knowledge—esoteric and wonder-working wisdom, because any knowing is directly related to the cosmic order itself."[19] In other words, ancient man, emerging from his cave, squints at the sunlight and marvels at the phenomena suddenly apparent to his untrained eyes. All that he sees is strange to him; nothing is adequately explained. The seasons, the weather, the cycle of life, all are mysteries. To master his surroundings and dull the sense of perpetual confusion in which he's mired, he turns to games. Play, writes Huizinga, is not mimetic—aping the natural order it observes—but methectic—creating order by imposing patterns of its own. "Culture," he observes, "arises in the form of play. . . . It is played from the very beginning. Even those activities which aim at the immediate satisfaction of vital needs—hunting, for instance—tend, in archaic society, to take on the play-form."[20]

Playing video games, we are all, for a moment, archaic once again. Because we are compelled not just to observe but to do, we begin each play as if emerging from our cave for the first time. We seek not only to adjust to our environment but also to achieve some sense of mastery, a sensation that transcends mere utilitarian needs. The video game industry learned this lesson quickly. In the medium's early days, in the mid-1970s, with games available solely in oversized wooden cabinets in public settings, good players, players who met the game's challenges and cleared levels quickly and effortlessly, were rewarded with additional turns. This was a staple design principle of pinball, an industry for which many of the early video game pioneers—including Nolan Bushnell, the founder of Atari—worked before going electronic. And it made perfect sense: time, after all, was money, and an extra turn was both, a useful gift guaranteed to motivate players to reach for their pockets. It did, but only to an extent. And then came *Space Invaders*.

Released in 1978 by the Japanese company Taito, the game was a well-designed but not extraordinary space-themed shooter. Revolving around rows of aliens descending with increasing speed, it was similar to several other games available at the time, with one notable exception: it recorded the player's high score. That in itself was sufficient to catapult *Space Invaders* into the video game pantheon, and its sales into the millions. But the breakthrough would not be complete until the following year when another popular game, *Asteroids*, took the concept of the high score to its logical end. First of all, unlike *Space Invaders*, *Asteroids* didn't offer those included on the high score list a free game; the record was a reward on its own. Even more radically, anyone who had achieved a high score was entitled not only to see the score registered on-screen, but also to enter one's initials into the game, to be kept there, presumably, in posterity or until another player beat the record. To motivate novice players, the game shipped programmed with fictional high scores, providing a hard-to-reach yardstick.[21]

The influence of the new, personalized high score was immense. Game magazines, such as *Nintendo Power* or *Sega Visions*, began to publish high scores, often in glossy pullout sections. In the summer of 1981, a man named Walter Day visited more than one hundred video game arcades across the United States, registering high scores; on February 9, 1982, he released the Twin Galaxies National Scoreboard, a database tracking video game high scores. The enthusiasm for the new concept was so great that Day's scoreboard began appearing regularly in a host of magazines all over the world. The notion, however, wasn't limited only to the trade publications; mainstream newspapers were swept up in the trend as well. North Carolina's *Chapel Hill News*, for example, ran a story on November 10, 1982, titled, "Resident Saves Earth, Claims World Record," about the efforts of a local seventeen-year-old boy to break the high score in the video game *Robotron*,[22] while the *San Francisco Examiner,* on September 6 of the same year, ran a similar story of another young man and another video game, this time called *Defender*.[23]

The ubiquity of the high score concept calls attention to a fundamental truth about video games. Players, to use Marxist terminology, were interested not in use-value but in exchange-value. A free game was a functional reward, but there were greater rewards; cash was strong, but glory stronger.

And there is no better conduit of glory than time. Unlike movies, say, which progress at a set pace, video game time is fluid. Players could do nothing but spend all their play time standing around and observing the game's scenery. There are no inherent scarcities to video game time—no film reels that need to be changed or plots that need to hurtle toward conclusion or TV time slots that need to be observed. In this abundance game designers found inspiration, creating, to use the poet Charles Bernstein's term, "an artificial economy of scarcity in a medium characterized by plenitude."[24] Therefore, games were programmed to be played in intervals of approximately thirty seconds each, with each quarter buying roughly three or four such segments. The game, then, was constantly interrupted, constantly played under an impending sense of doom, constantly influenced by an ominous sense of premature closure. Such a sensation, Bernstein noted, would not have been possible to manufacture if each quarter bought not a "turn," meaning a chunk of play that, although programmed in advance so that most players wouldn't be able to last very long, gave players the sensation that it was their skill alone that determined the duration of each play segment, but, say, a predetermined amount of time. "If your quarter always bought two minutes of play," Bernstein wrote, "the effect of artificial scarcity would largely disappear."[25]

In the late 1970s, however, as early gaming consoles like the Atari 2600 carried video games from darkened barrooms into living rooms, this system of premature closure manufactured by an artificial sense of scarcity no longer made sense. Without having to feed the machine quarters, designers had to construct new ways of regulating game time. It was no easy challenge. "A film ticket or video rental buys you just 90 or 120 minutes of 'media,' no extensions (as opposed to reruns) possible," Bernstein wrote. "Meanwhile, the home video game, by allowing longer play with greater skills, simulates the temporal economy of the arcade product while drastically blunting the threat of closure, since on the home version it costs nothing to replay."[26] With the average video game now taking approximately anywhere between twenty and forty hours to beat, video games have become the medium of superabundance, at least as far as time expenditure is concerned. With players now able to repeat the play experience ad infinitum, and with investment no longer measured in quarters but in minutes and hours and days, what enticement could game designers offer that would keep players engaged?

The answer was surprising. To capture and maintain the attention of players, designers soon learned, it was best to stay away from concrete rewards, goals, or anything else that reeked of progression and suggested the possibility of an impending end to the play experience. Rather than pack their games with nothing but levels, enemies, missions, and other manifestations of the concrete, game designers focused on nonessential items, virtual trinkets that have little impact on the game yet considerably open up the space of possibility for players. Mario's coins are an excellent example: in the early games in the massively popular series, golden coins were introduced and applied as a safety net of sorts—with each one hundred coins collected, the player received an extra life. By the time the franchise matured, however, its custodians realized that coins have a far greater potential to engage players. In *Wario World 4*, they dispatched Wario, the beloved cap-donning plumber's evil twin, to explain this logic bluntly: "For some reason, coins appear when you smash enemies! Don't think about it too hard, Einstein! There are some supernatural phenomena in the world that just can't be explained!!"

It is doubtful that Wario—or his creators—ever studied Maimonides, but his philosophical imprimatur is evident not only in the statement but in the game design principle it describes. The famed twelfth-century rabbi understood that faith was one thing and religion another. The former was based on belief in the existence of God, which was an ethereal concept. You could attempt to prove that God existed—Maimonides offered his own arguments, based largely on the notion that some force must have created the world *ex nihilo*—but that left you with very little knowledge of what that God was, or what God's plan was like, or what God's relationship was to you, the mortal creation. Humanity, therefore, was judged and punished by a creator about whom people knew little and whose ways were utterly mysterious. The only way to commune with the divine was to follow his decrees as laid out in the holy Torah. This notion rests, in part, on negative theology, or the idea that there are no positive, definitive statements we could make of God. Never able to say for certain that God exists, we should, instead, say that God doesn't not exist. God is an abstraction to us, and rather than ponder the imponderable we should focus on the earthly deeds God had prescribed.

The same logic applies in video games. Any concrete knowledge of the creator—the never-seen designer—is unavailable, and the creator's plan remains carefully concealed; to reveal it would be to spoil the pleasures of the game. Therefore, while some actions serve to directly promote the progression of the plot, many others are designed simply to sustain the inherent logic of the game as a hermetically sealed universe. Maimonides suggests that, being human, we'll never know God and therefore may as well focus on what's closer to us, on the intricate procedurals of religious life. Video games imply that as we're doomed to always exist in a system whose true nature—its algorithmic plan—we'll never fully know, we may as well focus less doggedly on attempts to beat the game—the closest we'll come to achieving anything resembling transcendence—and more on merely existing in it, which is made possible largely via interaction with nonessential items, like Mario's coins. Playing off of this idea, the series' designers expanded the role of coins considerably, applying them to allow players to discover new worlds and explore unlit corners of familiar ones. What this created, then, is a parallel universe: once players have tired of the linear nature of the game's main quest and its constant judgment of lives won and lost, players could retreat into a side quest of their own making and go off in search of the blue coin they needed to unlock one level or the red coin necessary to complete another. These were not essential tasks—in the game's internal logic, only the main quest mattered, and players could beat the game without exploring any of these distractions—but they were nonetheless invaluable in allowing players a mechanism through which to assert their sense of mastery over the world.

But this analysis fails to capture the magic of game play. It is akin to what the influential American Jewish rabbi Abraham Joshua Heschel called the sociological fallacy, or the secularist tendency to view religion as nothing more than a construct of rules and regulations leading to the creation of a convoluted and rather oppressive system. Instead, considered from the player's perspective, the potential for liberation hidden in this central feature of video games is revealed. Put simply, by allowing players the space, even within the strictures of an algorithmically confined universe, to construct their own plans in pursuit of what are, from a strictly utilitarian point of view, useless aims, video games give them one of modernity's greatest and rarest gifts: the ability to waste time.

Consider that in their infancy, video games, limited largely to single-screen interactions, offered nothing but a centralized quest. As the little man in the red cap—only later would he be called Mario—facing off the angry ape Donkey Kong, the player had to climb ladders, watch out for barrels and hammers and other flying bits of detritus, and make it to the top of the scaffolding in an effort to catch up with the foul-tempered primate and save the girl. In *Pac-Man*, the ravenous yellow fellow moved about a maze, chased by four ghosts whose patterns of movements were fixed, eating vitamins. The key to beating these games was sheer pattern recognition: you could time Donkey Kong's movements, calculate the trajectory of his weapons, and build up an unfailing rhythm that would keep you safe. You could map out the movements of Pac-Man's ghosts; even the supposedly randomized one, nicknamed Clyde, was less erratic than expected. With enough data, you could play forever. This is why both games end in a so-called kill screen—if you reached a certain level in the game, it simply activated a bug, lighting up the screen with pixilated carnage, no longer allowing play. When a player figured out the designer's secrets, the game world as such could no longer exist.

In these early games, then, the player's goal was always, metaphorically speaking, Godhood. If you only paid close enough attention, you could figure out the creator's intent, like those kabbalists who believed that all existence comprised secret but ultimately knowable patterns of numbers and letters. When the machines moved homeward, and the game grew more sprawling and complicated, this dynamic was no longer possible. As an arcade game, *Pac-Man* was a smashing success; as a cartridge for the Atari 2600 home console, it was a failure, with sales initially strong due to the franchise's renown but soon slowing to a trickle, leaving the company with an excess of 5 million units.[27] This, in part, was due to insufficient hardware; the home console was not yet as advanced as its bulkier ancestors. But it was also a result of a metaphysical quandary: with playtime now no longer restricted by an economy of coins, and therefore unlimited, where would players find a sense of emotional catharsis?

In waste.

Speaking of video games, parents, educators, and other responsible adults frequently and often sneeringly label them a waste of time. They are right, but for all the wrong reasons. Video games do waste time, but not mindlessly, never wantonly. They waste time in a way necessary to curb the otherwise rampant industriousness of developed capitalist societies, necessary to solve the central problem of the medium, namely how not to force humans, thoroughly analog creatures that we are, into digital mind-sets, bound by code and devoid of free will.

Long before the advent of digital media, Georges Bataille saw the problem arising. Ours, he wrote, was a society so obsessed with production that it has long exceeded its own capacities. We make and make and make, and, even at our most ravenous, lack the capacity to consume as much. This, wrote Bataille, could only lead to trouble. Comparing us to a bored and oppressed teenager whose father demands nothing but continuous and uncompromising rectitude, he wrote:

> In the most crushing way, the contradiction between current social conceptions and the real needs of society recalls the narrowness of judgment that puts the father in opposition to the satisfaction of his son's needs. This narrowness is such that it is impossible for the son to express his will. The father's partially malevolent solicitude is manifested in the things he provides for

his son: lodgings, clothes, food, and, when absolutely
necessary, a little harmless recreation. But the son does
not even have the right to speak about what really gives
him a fever; he is obliged to give people the impression
that for him no horror can enter into consideration. In
this respect, it is sad to say that conscious humanity
has remained a minor; humanity recognizes the right
to acquire, to conserve, and to consume rationally, but
it excludes in principle nonproductive expenditure.[28]

But nonproductive expenditure is necessary. Drawing on the
customs of early civilizations, and offering as an example the pot-
latch—the economic system favored by the indigenous people of
the Pacific Northwest, organized around the ceremonial giving
of excessive gifts—Bataille argued that these cultures understood
what ours dourly does not, namely that there was great symbolic
value in waste:

Connected to the losses that are realized in this way—
in the case of the "lost woman" as well as in the case of
military expenditure—is the creation of unproductive
values; the most absurd of these values, and the one
that makes people the most rapacious, is *glory*. Made
complete through degradation, glory, appearing in a
sometimes sinister and sometimes brilliant form, has
never ceased to dominate social existence; it is impossible to attempt to do anything without it when it is
dependent on the blind practice of personal or social
loss.[29]

The Hebrew Bible agrees. As the book of Leviticus begins, it
immediately sets itself apart from its predecessors by offering not
a story line but a list of regulations, beginning with the orders

of sacrifice. Curiously, as God conveys his orders to Moses, he begins not with what most of us perceive as the primary function of sacrificial offerings, namely repentance for sins, but with something much more concrete—burnt meat, says the Divine Being, smells nice. This is no trivial point: by ordering the Israelites to bring their unblemished animals to the priests for burning, God is prescribing an opportunity for all of his creations to get together, assert their sense of community, and enjoy the scent of roasted flesh. The bits about atonement come later; the prime purpose of ritualistic sacrifice, we're led to understand, is to bind people to each other and to the Lord. Nonproductive expenditure, then, becomes absolutely necessary, as the waste is what makes the Israelites, otherwise preoccupied merely by survival, stop and pay heed, conceiving of themselves as a community dedicated to a higher calling.

Talk to contemporary video game players and you'll hear them say more or less the same thing. They waste time gleefully, and not only as a form of escapism from the real world and its demands. They waste time because in wasting time they find a channel for the excessive dictates of production forced on each of them, on each of us, by e-mails that never cease pouring in and social networks in need of constant updates and a glut of information no human being can ever process. Players, savvy citizens of a digital landscape, know that they are constantly laboring and rarely compensated. They realize that their every tweet and Facebook status update is little more than content large corporations then sell to advertisers. Games offer a respite, an opportunity to step outside of the data stream for a moment by partaking in an activity that is beautifully unproductive. When you search for coins in *Mario*, say, or play Triple Triad, a card game,[30] in *Final Fantasy VIII*, or use your in-game scanner to catalog the flowers and plants you come across in *Metroid Prime*, you are working toward no productive goal in particular. You are not completing a quest, or achieving a goal, or doing anything that might be recorded on a high score board. Rather, you are living, as humans do, in the moment, choosing which preoccupations to pursue, abandoning the grand and unknowable scheme for the small and evident details.

Game producers are rapidly catching on to this idea. In 2006 Nintendo released *The Legend of Zelda: Twilight Princess*, a rich and sprawling game designed to showcase the then-new Nintendo Wii console; the game, side quests and all, took anywhere between forty and sixty hours to complete, a fact that struck most critics as impressive, even demanding. Exactly five years later, the next installment in the series, *The Legend of Zelda: Skyward Sword*, was released. To experience all of its offerings, players had to invest nearly one hundred hours, most of them on side quests and other distractions. This is not just excessiveness, the same faulty logic that perpetually pushes Hollywood to make movies more costly and louder. Rather, it is a design principle that betrays a deep understanding of why so many people spend so much time playing so many games. They—we—do so because games, while purely digital, conjure the ancient rhythms of our species. They understand that glory is more important to us than resolution. They know that we can live without precise knowledge of the architecture of our circumstances, but not without a sense of agency to affect them. They realize that story is one stratum of human life, but ritual another, deeper one. And video games, as we'll soon see, are closer in spirit to ritual than they are to any other human pursuit.

A Ballet of Thumbs

WHAT WE DO WHEN WE PLAY VIDEO GAMES

There's one question anyone who plays video games has come to dread: "What are you doing?" It's a terrifying question, and not only because it is very frequently asked in a particular tone that suggests the question is rhetorical and the asker judgmental. What's truly frightening about the question is that playing video games—like kneeling in prayer or making love or running a race or listening to music or any other heavily sensual and deeply emotional undertaking—is an experience that does not readily lend itself to description. The thrills it offers are airy, its joys ephemeral. And yet, to gain any real insight into the medium and its machinations, one must first take a controller to hand and play.

When I set out to do just that, I was struck by the innate difficulty of the task. I've been playing video games for the better part of three decades now, playing them every day since I was seven, thinking about them and writing about them and trying as well as I could to unlock the secrets of their charms. Learning to see video games anew, I thought of Marcel Proust's idiom that the real voyage of discovery consists not of seeking new landscapes but of having new eyes. Abandoning games for a few months—a palate cleanser, I imagined, a clean slate—I finally approached my beloved Nintendo and decided to observe myself as I played *The Legend of Zelda: Twilight Princess*, a relatively recent and innovative entry in a series I greatly love.

It took me no time at all to learn—to recall—that video games are primarily concerned with the acquisition of skill. As each game begins, almost without exception, the player undergoes a tutorial that presents the basics of the game's mechanics. There are, of course, many similarities between one game and the next, but as games are ranked, in large part, on the play experience they offer, and as that experience depends on innovative and immersive game play, it is vital to allow players the chance to slowly master the game's mechanics as they get further and further along.

Although he wasn't referring to video games in particular, this sort of skill acquisition is at the heart of the model set forth by Hubert Dreyfus.[1] Dreyfus assumed the French philosopher Maurice Merleau-Ponty's masterwork, *Phenomenology of Perception*, as his point of departure and focused his own model around two of Merleau-Ponty's key concepts: the intentional arc and the desire for or the drive toward maximal grip.[2]

The *intentional arc* concept argues that as an individual—or, in Merleau-Ponty's language, an agent—acquires a particular subset of knowledge or skills, those skills are retained not as ideated representations stored in the agent's mind and awaiting some contextual reawakening, but rather as increasingly fine-tuned inclinations to respond to the callings of increasingly fine-tuned perceptions of any given situation to which they relate. "The life of consciousness," wrote Merleau-Ponty, "cognitive life, the life of desire or perceptual life—is subtended by an 'intentional arc' which projects round about us our past, our future, our human setting, our physical, ideological and moral situation."[3] In other words, Merleau-Ponty claimed that as we acquire skills—or, in his language, "habits"—we are likely to encounter a growing number of temptations, invitations, and solicitations to immerse ourselves in situations that require our acquired habits. A kid who has just learned to ride her bike, for example, can't wait to take it out for a spin and is likely to find herself riding aimlessly, just to ride, tempted by her newfound mastery.

Similarly, Merleau-Ponty used the term *maximum grip* to describe the body's tendency to respond to such invitations in a way, in Dreyfus's words, that would "bring the current situation closer to the agent's sense of an optimal gestalt."[4] Having learned to ride her bike without wobbling or falling, the young rider asks herself what else she could do. She may then attempt to go faster, as fast as she could, or tilt her front wheel upward, or try to ride hands-free. Her nature is to want to hone her skill as much as she possibly can.

Drawing on the work of J. J. Gibson, the renowned psychologist of visual perception, Dreyfus added one more component to those constructing the intentional arc, namely an a priori acquaintance with or knowledge of cultural expectations. In his *The Ecological Approach to Visual Perception*,[5] Gibson argued that it is not only "natural" components that dictate our perception of and regulate our interaction with objects—namely the shape and qualities of things and our physical capacities to interact with them—but also a more complex network of preexisting knowledge. Seeing a mailbox and a letter, Gibson argues, is, in and of itself, not a sufficient clue to deciphering their usage; while they possess the physical qualities that make them compatible—the mailbox has a slot, the letter's size correlates perfectly to the size of that slot—and while we are certainly capable of picking up the letter and sliding it through the mailbox's slot, we must first be familiar with the postal service and its machinations if we wish to successfully interact with these two objects.[6]

Merleau-Ponty had similar ideas in mind when he fashioned one of his key concepts, that of embodiment:

> The body is our general medium for having a world. Sometimes it is restricted to the actions necessary for the conservation of life, and accordingly it posits around us a biological world; at other times, elaborat-

ing upon these primary actions and moving from their literal to a figurative meaning, it manifests through them a core of new significance: this is true of motor habits such as dancing. Sometimes, finally, the meaning aimed at cannot be achieved by the body's natural means; it must then build itself an instrument, and it projects thereby around itself a cultural world.[7]

Merleau-Ponty remained true to his formulation even when considering the acquisition of mental habits, as he believed body and mind were necessarily intertwined. A human being, he argued, had no tool other than the body with which to learn any skill or acquire any habit. "The analysis of motor habit as an extension of existence leads," he wrote, "to an analysis of perceptual habit as the coming into possession of a world. Conversely, every perceptual habit is still a motor habit and here equally the process of grasping a meaning is performed by the body."[8]

This idea of embodiment is evident to anyone who has ever observed a young boy play a video game. Long and wrongfully identified as the domain of that quintessentially passive being, the couch potato, video games are far more physical than we imagine. As the child plays a racing game, say, the prompt on the screen demands a sharp right turn. This is a mental stimulus requiring no other action from the child than a slight flick of the thumb, moving the control stick to the right and manipulating the car on screen accordingly. But watch the child, and you'll notice his entire body leaning right, as if he himself was making that turn, as if he was the driver, as if he were the car. The child can't help it: he has no other medium for having a world than his body. As he plays, he, like every other gamer, will use that body to go through the five stages of skill acquisition, described by Dreyfus: novice, advanced beginner, competent, proficient, and expert.[9] With these stages in mind I first entered the world of Hyrule, a beautiful and verdant kingdom threatened by an emergent evil force.

After a brief process of installation, which included connecting the proper cables to the television set and calibrating the wireless communication between the video game console and the control pad, I was ready to begin playing. The first and most discomforting discovery of a video game player is likely the correct grip required to hold the control pad. Unlike a television's remote control or a computer's mouse, both of which are gripped by the palm of one hand and depend upon the thumb or a finger or two to press their buttons, the video game control pad was designed to be held with both hands, with the pad's curvature fitting between the thumb and the index finger. The left hand's thumb must stay perpendicular to the control stick located on the pad's left-hand side, so that the stick presses against the carpometacarpal joint, allowing for maximum rapid rotation movement. The right hand's thumb, however, must be placed horizontal to the pad, just beneath a cluster of buttons it must spring and press when the occasion calls. Both index fingers rest on a lower platform containing two triggers, located at the forefront of the pad, a finger on each trigger.

The difficulties associated with such a grip are immense. As I rotated my left thumb in an effort to move my character around, I was tempted, at first, to replicate the same movement with my right. Similarly, as my right thumb was called upon to press buttons, the left often joined it, stupidly and without reason, pressing down on a resistant stick. The overall effect was disharmonious, as if a fundamental balance of the body's symmetry had been disturbed. This seemed particularly true as the left thumb moved mainly on a vertical axis while the right one was confined primarily to the horizontal.

As Dreyfus argued, the predominant feature of the novice stage is the breaking down of the task environment into "context-free features which the beginner can recognize without benefit of experience in the task domain."[10] As most contemporary video games require the player to master a wide array of skills and movements, as well as recognize key features of distinct environments and internalize a few significant guiding rules—and so as not to interrupt the flow of the game once the actual narrative has been set in motion, the lion's share of games feature an introduction of sorts, in which the protagonist, not yet presented with the quest that comprises the bulk of the game, meanders around the game environment and is taught the basic necessary skills. In war or sports games, this segment usually appears as a bona fide training session; *Zelda*, however, is an adventure game, and therefore presented no inherent opportunity to send the game's protagonist, Link, on a brief training spell.

Instead, the game began with Link exploring three distinct screens, representing his home, his ranch, and his native village. In each screen he was met by characters from the game who explained to him, in the form of on-screen textual dialogue (the game does not have embedded speech), how to perform a certain task. In his yard, for example, a little girl handed him a slingshot and informed him that in order to use it he must press a certain button and aim with the motion stick. This, of course, had a somewhat disorienting effect: to hear a character in the game refer to the mechanics of the hardware I, the player, was holding in my hand in the real world made me reflect on the fact that I was involved in game play, which, in turn, greatly undermined the suspension of disbelief required to successfully immerse oneself in all fictional narratives. I continued to play, however, as the narrative had not yet begun in earnest and as the emphasis at this stage of the game was placed on correctly executing a handful of distinct movements and a few more combinations thereof.

Again, I was confronted with the problem of hand coordination. My left thumb controlled Link's movement, and as such mainly tilted backward and forward. My right thumb had to navigate between four buttons, each of which made Link perform a different task: one made him swing his sword, another made him dash or jump, and the two buttons just above them, reserved for controlling weapons I had yet to acquire, did nothing. More than once during the training period I found myself walking toward an opponent and, with a swing of the sword in mind, became frustrated when my right thumb, landing on the wrong button, produced a wrong outcome or no outcome at all. Often, my response to such mishaps would be to tighten my grip on the pad, as if the pad was not a collection of buttons controlling Link's movements by assigning value to each button but the thing itself, the real sword, an object I needed only to grasp more firmly if I were to master its potentialities. The result was increased perspiration and excessive muscular tension, and I was soon devoting nearly as much attention to being aware of my nervous tendencies as to my attempts at mastering the game's movements.

During this time I was also aware of the importance of the eyes in guiding my hands. At first, trying to master Link's movements, I kept my eyes on the screen and moved my thumbs and index fingers in ways I hoped were correct. The more mistakes I made, however, the more I found myself peeking down at my hands nearly every time a move was required that involved the combination of more than one or two elements (buttons, levers, triggers, etc.). Teaching himself how to play jazz piano, David Sudnow experienced the same phenomenon:

> Anyone who's witnessed or been a beginning pianist or guitarist learning chords notices substantial initial awkwardness. Lots of searching and looking are first required. The chord must be detected as a sequence of named notes with a look that reviews the terrain up and down, finding the chord as a serial ordering of

these and those particularly identified tones, going left
to right or right to left, consulting the rules to locate
the places. Then some missing ones in the middle are
found. And along with such looking are hands that
behave correspondingly.[11]

This visual and manual collaboration continued for the better
part of an hour, the time period it took me to master the game's
basic controls. Throughout that time, the unfurling narrative on
the screen, minimal as it was in the training stage, interested me
very little. I paid no attention to characters or graphics, to dia-
logues or settings. My attention was focused solely on my hands.

In Dreyfus's terms, I was entering the second stage, that of the
advanced beginner, which focused on deepening my comfort
with my newly acquired skills while introducing a nonsituational
element, namely an entryway into the task's contextual environment.[12] In the world of the game, I needed to abandon the initial
training stage and embark on the quest that would constitute the
bulk of the game's narrative. This step, of course, required a relative degree of comfort with the manual motions necessary to control the game, as the eyes were now required to concentrate on the
on-screen content.

My first reaction to this change was to postpone for as long
as possible any concrete interaction. As I began to play I guided
Link throughout the game environment, spending as much time
as I could acquainting myself with each screen I visited prior to
interacting with objects or other characters. Once such interaction began, I noticed that I resorted to my novice self, becoming
less and less concerned with the story and focusing instead on the
mechanics of my movement. As I approached each interaction, I
stopped, repositioned my hands on the pad to ensure a good grasp
(although I no longer tightened my grip whenever frustration set
in), and proceeded to converse, fight, or perform whatever task

was at hand. Such interactions occurred for me, not as an integral part of the gaming experience, which I perceived at that point as consisting mainly of allowing Link and me to explore the game's environment, but as interruptions to the narrative flow.

This response is likely for anyone reared on passive consumption of dramatic narratives. Even without contemplating the theories of interactivity discussed in the previous chapter, it took no stretch of the imagination to realize that the demand for active agency disrupted the passivity with which one is accustomed to consuming narratives, primarily on television and in films. I now realized that, as an advanced beginner, I nurtured a duality that I could not shake, alternating between competing yet complementary personae. The first is that of the Watcher. Concerned with visual elements, colors, shapes, and so forth, the Watcher seeks limited movement, lays the control pad on his knees, and taps it gently whenever necessary. He listens intently to the game's soundtrack and is actively trying to decipher its topography, making a map of the game's world in his head. He is similarly curious about the functionality of each of the game world's objects: cautiously entering a brook, for example, to examine how Link's movement is influenced by water, or swinging a sword at a tree to see whether any beneficial result ensues, he timidly tests out each item that is revealed before him. Whenever possible, he proceeds with caution, watches, and waits. His antithesis is the Doer. Raising the pad and holding it in midair, the Doer moves his thumbs and index fingers at an ever faster, increasingly more urgent pace. His heart beats fast, his pulse quickens, he's likely to sweat more and salivate. He hears nothing but the din of buttons depressed and recoiling back to position. He's the dominant one whenever an enemy appears on screen and combat is required; he's not one for cognitive alertness, just for reflexes. But when the action dies down, the contemplative persona once again regains control.

The transition between these two modes was jarring. When,

for example, I strolled through the fields of Hyrule on one occasion, happily swinging my sword at the overgrown wheat, curious as to what might lie underneath, I was suddenly attacked by a sharp-beaked albatross. This interaction, to be sure, required basic combat skills: pressing the left-hand trigger with my left index finger to activate my shield, repeatedly pressing a button with my right thumb to swing my sword, and using my left thumb to guide Link toward the malicious bird so as to ensure maximal damage. As I was startled by my foe while focusing on learning the dynamics of my environment—not all objects in any given screen were interactive—I was in a passive, cognitive mind-set; it took me nearly fifteen seconds to overcome the sudden jolt of having been attacked, readjust the position of the pad, and switch mind-sets to the active, manual-centric one.

This readjustment itself is indicative of just how much this shift startled me. Physically, there was no justification whatsoever to holding the pad in midair and pointing it at the screen as opposed to letting it rest on one's lap. That I instinctively associated the former with action and the latter with exploration, however, proved that I was still not free of my original misperception, the one that made me confuse the pad with Link's sword and drove me to tighten my grip in response. Raising the pad in midair and aiming it at the screen appealed to me on some unconscious level, as I clearly associated such a move with increasing the efficiency of my tool. It was also a physical response more substantial than merely pressing buttons, a fact that calmed me somewhat; I was being attacked, I told myself quietly, and I raised my pad in response like a shield. I was being proactive.

For all of the aforementioned reasons, the advanced beginner stage of skill acquisition was exhausting. The constant shift in sensibilities, the divergent traits each mode required, and the realization that I was still not rid of the nonsensical feeling of transference when it came to my tools all made game play at this stage highly unenjoyable. Whereas I completed the introductory stage in one consecutive hour, I found myself, immediately upon beginning to play the game in earnest, playing for increasingly shorter intervals with increasingly long breaks between each segment, eventually letting nearly a week pass before picking up the controller once more.

Fortunately for me, the conventions of game design recognize the problematic nature of the advanced beginner stage and adjust the opening stages of games accordingly: before too long, I completed the game's first major task, defeating a boss and unlocking a bit of the plot's mystery. Encouraged by this external validation of mastery I was ready to play on, hoping that further play would prove easier. Any such desire, however, soon proved to be premature. Describing the third stage of skill acquisition, Dreyfus details both the obstacles to and the solutions for attempting to reconcile situational and nonsituational components and integrating essentially mechanical skills into a more complex context:

> With more experience, the number of potentially relevant elements of a real-world situation that the learner is able to recognize becomes overwhelming. At this point, since a sense of what is important in any particular situation is missing, performance becomes nerve-wrecking and exhausting, and the student might wonder how anybody ever masters the skill. To cope with this problem and to achieve competence, people learn, through instruction or experience, to adopt a hierarchical perspective. First they must devise a plan, or choose a perspective, that then determines which elements of the situation are to be treated as important and which ones can be ignored. By restricting themselves to only a few of the vast number of possibly relevant features and aspects, decision-making becomes easier.[13]

After completing the game's first task I enthusiastically continued to play, certain that my improvement was imminent. Yet as soon as the second task began, a sense of frustration sank in, a dark cloud that grew thicker with each screen played. First, the frequency of being attacked by hostile interactive creatures became much higher; in the first stage of the game I clocked an interaction, on average, every thirty-one seconds, but the second task presented a challenge approximately every seventeen seconds, the game now replacing each slain creature with an identical one within a few moments, thereby making lingering in any one place inadvisable. Additionally, the number of screens now available for exploration became much greater; to the three initial screens of the introductory phase were added a dozen more, rendering futile any attempt to construct an accurate mental map of the game world and its geography. With cognitive and manual demands both increasing, I became increasingly exasperated. Unlike my emotion at the previous stage of skill acquisition, however, my frustration was now aimed solely at myself. I was enough of a skilled player to no longer blame the game for being too hard or otherwise inadequate; I knew better. Whatever I couldn't do right was solely my own fault.

Experiencing that frustration so poignantly described by Dreyfus, I began to question my ability to ever master the game. As the game now constituted a major part of my mental life over the course of a few weeks, I was reluctant to set it aside; on the other hand, I was also reluctant to believe that any significant improvement in my abilities would manifest itself suddenly and was unhappy with the notion of continuing to pursue a stressful and unrewarding task. Still, I decided to persevere and sought some structure to help me play more propitiously.

My first step was to seek external instruction. Until that point, my play experience existed regardless of any frame of reference unrelated to my immediate actions. But as I was failing to execute these actions in an integrated manner, I decided to study the brief video clips the console plays once a player logs off of a game and allows the system to stand idle. These clips show preexisting, computer-generated fight scenes, and I hoped they would give me not only a glimpse into some of the screens that lay ahead, but also, and more importantly, what perfect execution of play might look like.

For more than an hour I watched computer-controlled Link prance about on the screen. I looked for telling tales in his movement: Did he break left or right during a sword attack? At which point before reaching an obstacle did he leap? How often did he use the dash function, and how often did he just walk? I was searching for minute, mechanical clues, hoping that if I were able to break down his movements into individually recognized portions I would later be able to replicate it in sequence. That, I thought, was how complicated movements were often taught in the real world; as a child, studying martial arts, I was taught how to high-kick, with the instructor demonstrating each stage of the kick separately and urging us to practice each motion separately before putting together the complete kick itself. As I was unable to pause the pictures on the screen, I watched repeatedly, training myself to focus on small portions of the movement each time, taking copious notes in the process. Finally, I was certain that I had gleaned at least a few insights from this observation.

I was wrong. As I attempted to replicate computer-controlled Link's movement, I realized that my attempts, although sufficiently faithful to what I had seen just a short while before, produced inconsistent results. Dashes would sometimes hasten and at other times hinder movement, jumps would come too soon or not soon enough, sword swings landed now on the right side and then on the wrong. In short, emulation of what I had perceived to be a perfect state of play, a state of play independent of human agency, proved to be a failure. An alternative system was necessary.

As I could not reform my own movement, I decided to try and focus my efforts on adhering as closely as I could to the game's own design structure. Knowing that every game comprises various tasks, levels, or sections that the player must complete before finishing the game, I decided to abandon my aspirations to achieve a harmonious state of control over Link and his movements—to abandon the quest for the Merleau-Pontian "maximum grip," the feeling of proficiency with and comfort in the game environment—and reimagine the game instead as a series of interconnected though ultimately independent tasks that I had to complete. In other words, instead of striving to achieve proficiency to a degree that Link's actions would become second nature to me, and engage with the game world in a fluent and coherent manner, I now stressed my inability to seamlessly guide Link through the game world by breaking down that world into stand-alone challenges. At this point, of course, the game's narrative dissolved; focused as I was on surviving the next screen, I was much less concerned with the overall arc of the story. To borrow imperfect examples from other media, I was solving a puzzle, not watching a movie. To further train myself to perceive the game in this way, I got in the habit of pausing the game every few minutes to save my progress to the console's hard drive, a habit that greatly interrupted game play.

To better succeed at my current task, however, saving the progress I'd made on the game's hard drive often was insufficient. No longer able to freely explore the game's screens, I set about to draw a real map to augment and eventually replace the faulty mental one on which I had toiled. Paying little attention to scale or accuracy, I grabbed a sheet of paper and a pen and drew a brief sketch representing an approximation of the game's world: Link's house, his ranch and his village; Hyrule's fields and the adjacent mines, the Forest Castle and Death Mountain. I used arrows to indicate which screen led into which, and crosses to note where important objects or characters, such as a parrot that sold necessary goods, were to be found.

As I gradually advanced from one screen to another and learned in greater detail the nature of the tasks ahead of me, I wrote down a short description of each task I encountered. The result was a brief and enigmatic to-do list: free the monkey, use him to cross the bridge, get the key, open the door, get the heart container, and so forth. While I was paying a modicum of attention to my surroundings, I was more interested in my map than in the actual environment portrayed on the screen. I soon came to trust the map more than I did my own sense of orientation; if I wondered whether a particular screen might lead to another, I never ventured to try without first glimpsing at my map. This strategy greatly reduced all stress associated with my previous attempts to gain cognitive mastery over the game world; that world, I was now content to realize, was not mine to discover, but a prefabricated construct I had to put together piecemeal, in short and rather mindless bursts. In other words, I was not truly a subject, at least not in the pure Cartesian sense; I was no thought and all extension.

While I say much more later on about the question of subjectivity and its relation to video games, this third stage of skill acquisition brought to mind an interesting and common grammatical confusion that seemed to capture perfectly the position one holds when playing a video game. In a sentence, the grammatical agent and the grammatical subject are often seen as interchangeable; this is erroneous, however, as agency is formed solely on the basis of relation to the verb, or the action, while subjectivity is formed according to the sentence's flow of information, word order, construction, and so on. In the sentence, "The girl broke the glass," for example, the girl is both agent and subject; but rewrite the sentence as, "The glass was broken by the girl," and the girl remains the agent but is no longer the subject, as the subject now becomes the glass. It occurred to me, while playing in an interrupted and episodic manner, that the architecture as compared to the grammar of video games required a permanent distinction between agent and subject; the player may retain agency, but the subject forever remains the game itself, designed, as it was, by someone else who is not a participant in the play experience and to whose logic and whim the player, agent or not, must succumb.

Still, my newfound method produced great results. I was completing task after task, finding my way around, thanks to the ever-growing map, with relative ease. As far as the manual side of my experience was concerned, here, too, I noticed change; while I still required a brief pause prior to engaging in interaction, my response time now dropped to a few seconds, and while engaged in the interaction itself I was now comfortable enough with the dynamics of movement to interact thoughtlessly and fluently. I achieved the state that, borrowing a popular and common phrase often favored by athletes, computer game scholar Steven Poole dubbed "muscle memory": "One of the reasons you feel so fluidly involved," he wrote of the play experience, "is that your muscle memory has taken over the mechanical business of operating buttons, joysticks, triggers, or foot-pedals."[14]

Achieving muscle memory did not come about consciously. There was no particular moment in the play experience in which I felt a line being crossed, like the distant purr of a car engine when gears are shifted. Rather, only by closely analyzing video recordings of my play sessions did I observe this phenomenon transpiring. Suddenly, I noticed, I was no longer looking at my hands, as my thumbs and index fingers had by now committed to memory the exact location of each of the buttons they were required to press or the sticks they were called upon to manipulate. I also noticed that I moved my fingers about the control pad much more rapidly. During the introductory stage of the game, I clocked my average sword shift, an action which required the left thumb to navigate the movement stick and the right one to press the button, at three and a half seconds; the same movement, once muscle memory set in, took approximately three-quarters of one second. And while I wasn't able, even after repeated viewings of my play sessions, to pinpoint a specific moment in which muscle memory had set in, it became clearly evident after approximately three hours into the third stage of skill acquisition, or just over ten hours of total game play. At this stage, paraphrasing the recent findings of some researchers,[15] the game demanded less and less constant cognitive attention.

At this stage of the play experience, however, I became mindful of another significant phenomenon. I was well aware that a successful video game requires a certain level of identification between player and character; if I cared little or not at all about the land of Hyrule and the fate of its denizens, if I harbored no concrete feelings toward Link, how could I be expected not only to endure hours and hours of play but also to assume responsibility for a fictional character and aspire to improve my skills so as to better guide him through his travails? I assumed, however, that such a level of identification was a cognitive factor and therefore occurred at the point in the game at which the cognitive faculties were most at ease. Seeking to measure identification was a tricky task; how was I to tell if I cared for Link and, furthermore, if my empathy for him had increased in any way? My most efficient tool, I decided, would be language; as soon as I started playing *Zelda*, I began keeping a log in which I recorded various events that occurred throughout the game and the time at which they happened. Looking at these entries in retrospect, I hoped, would allow me to measure my degree of emotional investment, tracking noticeable changes in tone, word choice, length of entries, and any other indication that my own attitude toward my on-screen avatar was shifting in any discernable direction. Figure 1 on page 48 shows select entries from the log:

The table indicates a few crucial shifts. I began by registering the event descriptions in the log in a perfunctory way, focusing on how things were done: the goats, I noted, were herded in a certain manner, the falcon summoned from a certain place. I recorded what happened. I attributed every action in the game to Link, viewing him as the game's acting agent. Shortly before the advanced begin-

FIGURE 1

VARYING DESCRIPTIONS AS A FUNCTION OF SKILL ACQUISITION STAGE

Total Playing Time (in hours, minutes)	Skill Acquisition Stage	Event Description
1:16	Novice	Link herds goats by chasing them into the stable on horseback.
2:23	Novice	Link learns to summon the falcon; tall buildings preferable for such activity.
4:55	Advanced Beginner	Link runs out of oil for lantern, returns to parrot, buys more.
5:33	Advanced Beginner	Link frees first monkey by dashing into cage.
6:58	Advanced Beginner	Link acquires map of first dungeon; this should help.
7:41	Competent	Beat second boss; nasty. Got boomerang.
10:12	Competent	Stuck in dumb, dusty town. Burned down a house.
12:04	Competent	Figured out how to solve windmill puzzle. I rock!

ner phase ended, however, I noted that a map obtained "should help," yet it is unclear whether the object would benefit Link, as the character in the game, or myself as the player, as I obviously would be required to consult the map in order to determine Link's movements. Soon after crossing over into the competent stage, references to Link disappeared altogether. There was now no subject or agent to my sentences. They began with a verb. And while I was still mainly focused on describing the unfolding of the game's narrative, keeping my sentences short and the details minimal, I was now including adjectives. The second boss was "nasty." The town "dusty" and, even more strikingly, "dumb." Both of these adjectives capture, I believe, a peculiar state of mind. Obviously, I was not physically present in the town, and "dusty" is an inaccurate description; having revisited the town after taking the aforementioned note, I noticed that nothing in particular about the way the town was graphically rendered suggests dust—no particles floating in the air, as is sometimes the case—apart, perhaps, from a somewhat yellowish color palette. For whatever reason, then, I captured the color scheme in an adjective that conveyed more than a physical description. I did not enjoy spending time in the town and therefore thought it dusty. And dumb: this is a much more blatant, and perhaps more telling, example of my feeling clear emotion toward an element of the game, something that did not happen for the first few hours of game play. Finally, two hours after a muscle memory of sorts first became apparent in my play, I used the one word to describe Link that I had previously consciously avoided: I.

Describing a puzzle I had solved, I once again allowed for a show of emotion, noting with self-satisfaction, "I rock!" Before I began writing in the log, I debated to whom I should attribute the agency in the game, and decided that Link was the appropriate choice; while I pressed buttons and manipulated control sticks, he was on the screen, running and jumping and swinging his sword.

And since I did not feel that he and I were one, I decided it would be more instructive if I, like a disinterested observer standing on the sidelines, described the unfolding of the narrative in terms of what happened to Link. Twelve hours into the game, however, I unwittingly broke my own rule; after having dispensed with Link altogether in my sentences, I now commented that it was I, not he, who deserved credit for solving a particularly tough puzzle. It was, in other words, I, not he, who was the agent in charge.

The question of identification between player and character is one that has received much theoretical attention, yet little of what has been written accurately captures the brittle and elusive nature of this relationship. The first studies concerning the correlation between identity development and communication processes can be traced to the 1930s, and particularly to the work of psychologist G. H. Mead. In his *Mind, Self, and Society*,[16] Mead argued that communication was the prism through which an individual becomes conscious of both others and oneself. According to Mead, the process of identification with the other is achieved as the self takes on the role of the other, an undertaking, he suggested, that is accomplished via communication and that instills in the self the ability to develop empathy for the other and at the same time a clear perception of the self. While such a process, Mead argued, was once limited to direct experience, mass media now enabled anyone to take on the role of even a distant or nonexistent other and thereby become integrated into society. A similar thread thrived with the advent of television, when several studies[17] suggested that viewers strongly identified with the fictional characters on screen, often resorting to role playing when the identification was particularly strong. The field of study of identification with television characters is rich and vast: Ellis, Streeter, and Engelbrecht,[18] for example, found that identification with television characters extended beyond the viewing experience, often prompting people to compose their own views according to views they thought might be held by their favorite television characters, while Reeves and Nass[19] found that people's interactions with media were guided by the same principles as would govern interpersonal interactions.

When identification studies migrated, in the late 1980s, from television to video games, attention was paid mainly to measuring time invested in playing video games versus that devoted to watching television. Yet those few studies that looked at identification with characters[20] found different effects than those associated with television. In an early study of video games that, sadly, has not been paralleled or expanded since it was written more than two decades ago, Gary Selnow claimed that video games' interactivity allowed players to become "a member of the cast" of the game,[21] thereby creating a different, and stronger, identification with the game's characters than television viewers were likely to develop with the characters in their programs. Another pair of researchers, McDonald and Kim, studied the subject of identification in relation to video games, providing questionnaires containing both closed- and open-ended questions to 303 elementary and high school students from New York State. In one case, the students were asked to describe their ideal selves, their actual selves, and their favorite video game characters. Their results appear in Figure 2 on page 52.

"The highest peaks throughout the sample are associated with ideal self—game character comparisons, suggesting some support for the notion that these concepts are somewhat similar in the players' minds,"[22] McDonald and Kim wrote. Still, their study, like Selnow's and virtually any other study on the subject, approached the question of identity from the perspective of the social self rather than exploring the dynamics of agency and the fine mechanics of the interaction between player and character. A cautious step in that direction was taken by James Paul Gee; in his chapter titled "Learning and Identity: What Does It Mean to Be a

FIGURE 2

SELF, IDEAL SELF, AND FAVORITE GAME CHARACTER

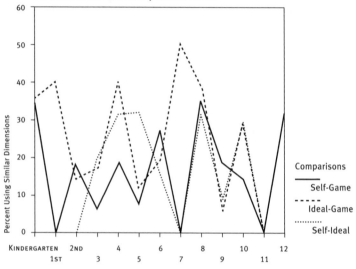

Percent of Players Using Similar Dimensions in Describing Their Self, Ideal Self, and Favorite Game Character by Grade in School

Source: McDonald and Kim, "When I Die, I Feel Small," 251.

Half-Elf?"[23] Gee described his experience playing a character named Bead Bead in a role-playing game called *Arcanum*. The play experience, he claimed, immediately constructs three distinct yet intertwined identities, which he called the virtual, the real, and the projective. In the first case, he wrote, "The stress is on the virtual character Bead Bead acting in the virtual world of Arcanum (though I am 'playing/developing' her)."[24] The second, respectively, stressed "the real-world character James Paul Gee playing Arcanum as a game in real time (though Bead Bead is the tool through which I operate the game)."[25] Finally, the third identity, labeled projective to connote both Gee's projecting of his values and desires into the virtual character of Bead Bead and his perception of Bead Bead as "one's own project in the making,"[26] emphasized "the interface between—the interactions between—the real world person and the virtual character."[27] As is suggested by the title of her article, "Who Am We?" Sherry Turkle suggested a similar approach, speaking of a "multiple but integrated identity."[28]

Yet the aforementioned studies, conducted mainly by cognitive scientists with limited long-term experience in game playing, assumed identification and the construction of identity to be a cognitive process, in which the individual identities of player and character are actively dismantled, combined, and reassembled. Such an approach, however, ignored a key element of video games, namely their physicality: by assuming a purely cognitive process, Turkle, Gee, et al. disregarded fundamental elements of video game design, history (the medium, after all, was born of reflex-sharpening devices commissioned by the military), and hardware (with physical interaction between player and machine being an area of growing innovation). Furthermore, they ignored a key aspect of the phenomenology of video games: the game play experience consists at least equally of manual components like pressing buttons as it does of cognitive components like making decisions. A 2006 survey of 420 professional gamers—individuals who earn a living playing in video game tournaments—confirmed this duality. When asked in an open-ended question to name the most positive and enjoyable elements of game play, participants named "improve reflexes," a purely physical notion, as one of the seven most attractive characteristics of the play experience.[29] What I refer to as the cognitive approach also excludes Dreyfus's findings pertaining to skill acquisition, which show that emotional identification with any task involving a degree of manual mastery, a good definition of the core video game playing experience, occurs only after a modicum of proficiency has been achieved, namely only once an individual is trained in the motions associated with the particular skill set the player is trying to acquire.[30]

As my own experience with the world of *Zelda* continuously demonstrated, cognitive awareness was reduced and automatic functions increased the greater my own mastery of the game became. Now many hours into the game, and having accomplished slightly more than half of the tasks required in order to complete the game's main quest, I began to notice a vast shift in my approach to the game. While, for the duration of the first few tasks, I adhered to a rigid structure, saving my progress often and breaking up the game's narrative into small, stand-alone tasks, I was now playing in a wholly linear, fluid way, allowing the game's narrative to unfold uninterrupted. Interactions with characters, once the source of much anxiety, were now effortless; in battles I would perform sidesteps and backflips, jabs and combo attacks, each of which demanded the simultaneous manipulation of the movement stick and at least two buttons. Even more encouragingly, I did not contemplate these moves in advance, but rather performed them instinctively, stopping to reflect on my actions only in retrospect if at all. I no longer raised the control pad when such an interaction came; instead, the pad remained resting on my lap at all times. Still, a major shift in body motion occurred: observing the video recordings, I noticed that a movement of my left thumb, for example, was often accompanied by movement of my left arm and shoulder, and every pulling of a trigger with my right index finger invited my body to tilt to the right in its entirety. In other words, I was no longer rigid, grasping the control pad tightly whenever a stressful situation occurred, but rather undulating according to the movements of my digits, allowing my entire body to follow the rhythmic clues provided by my fingers. The result was an odd shadow dance, in which I seemed to imitate Link's on-screen movements, leaning forward when he ran or dashed and swinging my hips when he swung his sword at an opponent. Often enough, directly after a particularly eventful interaction, I would catch myself in the midst of this strange dance and, becoming aware of myself, resume my calm, upright position on the couch. This happened in cycles: dance, awareness, calm, repeat.

Aron Gurwitsch, a philosopher and onetime teacher of Merleau-Ponty's, referred to this condition as a *state of absorption* and deemed it the paragon of immersion in any given activity, from the commonplace to the highly specialized. He wrote:

> What is imposed on us to do is not determined by us as someone standing outside the situation simply looking on at it; what occurs and is imposed are rather prescribed by the situation and its own structure; and we do more and greater justice to it the more we let ourselves be guided by it, i.e., the less reserved we are in immersing ourselves in it and subordinating ourselves to it. We find ourselves in a situation and are interwoven with it, encompassed by it, indeed just "absorbed" into it.[31]

Elaborating on Gurwitsch's notion, Merleau-Ponty was more specific in locating the focal point of immersion not in a cognitive process—that, to him, was an impossibility, as every process of mere observation was tantamount to Gurwitsch's "standing outside the situation simply looking at it"—but in the more concrete realm of the body. "A movement is learned when the body has understood it," he wrote, "that is, when it has incorporated it into its 'world,' and to move one's body is to aim at things through it; it is to allow oneself to respond to their call, which is made upon it independently of any representation."[32]

My experience at this stage of playing *Zelda* closely correlated to Merleau-Ponty's observations. With my body becoming freer to incorporate itself into the game play experience, and with my manual dexterity sufficient enough to allow for seamless play, I was now playing primarily through my fingers. An interesting question that remains, however, is that of the visual elements in video games. Obviously, being a visual medium and played on television sets or computer screens, video games must always strive to strike a balance between catering to the eye and the hand. As I played, I became aware of a direct ratio between the predominance of the hand versus that of the eye and the level of proficiency achieved; the better I became at performing the ballet of thumbs, manipulating Link as he ran and slashed and jumped, the less I needed to look at the screen. Of course, very few video game players would ever close their eyes altogether and give in to sheer movement, although a slew of recent games designed by and for blind gamers prove that even visual-heavy genres, like fighting games, can be played, literally, by ear, with the screen remaining dark and nothing but sound providing the player with the necessary cues. But the more I played, the more comfortable I was relying solely on peripheral vision to collect all the visual prompts and cues I needed to progress. I was now gleaning nothing but the most essential information from the screen, and then allowing my fingers to guide me through the interaction. And I was hardly alone: quoting the biography of basketball great Larry Bird, for example, Dreyfus discussed a similar phenomenon. "[A lot of the] things I do on the court are just reactions to situations," Bird wrote. "A lot of times, I've passed the basketball and not realized I've passed it until a moment or so later."[33]

David Sudnow, in a now largely outdated study of the first generation of video game arcade machines, discovered a similar shifting balance of power between eyes and hands. Documenting in detail the many hours he'd devoted to playing *Breakout*, an early ancestor of today's ubiquitous *Brick Breaker*, Sudnow, too, noticed the shift in the hierarchal nature between the faculties as he became a better player. "At first it felt like my eyes told my fingers where to go," he wrote. "But in time I knew the smooth rotating hand motions were assisting the look in turn, eyes and fingers in a two-way partnership."[34] Later on in the account, he admits that what at first consisted of gluing his eyes to the ball[35] soon became largely a manual motion, and that, at his new stage of mastery, "peripheral vision sufficed."[36] Even later, he claimed that his eyes would rove across the screen, looking now not so much at the places where the ball was falling but rather at the places where the ball was likely to fall in the immediate future; the ball being small and the paddle rather large, and the game consisting of only one screen, there were only so many distinct locations for the paddle to occupy, and Sudnow found that once his hands took over the mechanics of game play, his eyes were free to assess the possibilities. "The eyes," he added, "could plan."[37]

While Sudnow's account fits well with the narrow game environment of *Breakout*, a more complex game, one including many screens and a multitude of objects that require varying, differentiated, and interactive responses, the capacity of the eye to plan, and therefore to participate in the play process in a way that is anything but perfunctory, is greatly diminished. Manipulating Link across screens, my eyes had no incentive to wander across the game's terrain, surveying its outlines and proposing possible courses for future action. Rather, with the play experience flowing and the thumbs and index fingers in control of Link, my eyes found a convenient spot at the screen's center from which they could collect, aggregate, and transmit nothing but the necessary data to the busy manual mechanism now in charge.

As soon as this flow was in place, I became curious about its nature. While the primacy of the hands was clear to me, I wondered what, if anything, about the inherent architecture of the game enabled the flow to persist; in other words, what was it about the game that facilitated the state of absorption in which I was now immersed? And, in order to measure the flow, I had to interrupt it. Throughout the course of five one-hour-long play sessions, each occurring two days apart and taking place well into the proficiency stage, I requested an assistant to interrupt my play at agreed-upon intervals. The interruptions, five per session, occurred at intervals of roughly twenty minutes and consisted of the assistant asking me to pause the game for a second so that he could ask me a series of simple mathematical questions, guaranteeing that my cognitive faculties would be, for a brief while, transported entirely out of the world of the game and into the math problems at hand. I also instructed the assistant to observe my play closely and ensure that approximately half of his interruptions took place when Link was at an uneventful point in the game—running through a field, say, or commuting from one screen to another—while the other half was timed to coincide with highly interactive points in the narrative, such as major battle scenes or complicated puzzles. Once I resumed play, I would verbally comment on my difficulty in returning to the aforementioned state of absorption and ask my assistant to verify these statements by observing my on-screen performance as well as my body language. This experiment was designed to test the assumption made by some phenomenologists—most notably Merleau-Ponty, Dreyfus, and Gurwitsch—as well as philosophers like Martin Heidegger, regarding the nonrepresentational nature of learning and experience, namely the claim that knowledge is produced not through deliberate contemplation but simply through repetitive practice. I coded my findings as shown in Figure 3, with Roman numerals chronicling the individual interruption in each session, E connoting an eventful point at the narrative, and NE connoting a noneventful point. My own responses regarding difficulty at resuming play were measured in three increments: minimal, medium, and maximal.

As Figure 3 shows, the eventfulness of the game's narrative had little effect on the ease with which I immersed myself back in the game, while the duration of play prior to the interruption had a significant effect. The longer I played, and the more immersed I

FIGURE 3

INTERRUPTION OF PLAY AND ITS CORRELATION TO NARRATIVE
AND DURATION OF PLAY

Session	Interruption / Nature of Play	Difficulty at Resuming Play
1	I/NE II/E III/E IV/E V/NE	Minimal Minimal Medium Medium Maximal
2	I/E II/NE III/NE IV/E V/E	Minimal Minimal Minimal Medium Medium
3	I/NE II/NE III/NE IV/E V/E	Minimal Medium Medium Maximal Maximal
4	I/E II/NE III/NE IV/NE V/E	Minimal Minimal Medium Medium Medium
5	I/NE II/NE III/E IV/E V/E	Minimal Medium Medium Maximal Maximal

was in the game, the more disruptive the interruption. Interruptions during uneventful lulls occurring well into the session were, for the most part, considerably more disruptive than interruptions during eventful moments occurring relatively shortly after I'd begun playing. The game's eventfulness, in other words, seemed to matter very little; the amount of time invested in play was the only meaningful variable.

These observations, of course, are far from empirical. Although replicating the experiment many times with students yielded similar results, such findings are still a long way from telling us anything definitive. But they strongly suggest that much of the focus on games has been thoroughly misguided. By failing to pay much attention to the play experience itself—accounts such as my own and Sudnow's are exceedingly rare—and by concentrating instead on questions of aesthetics, narrativity, and other criteria familiar from other art forms, game scholars have provided much insight into the place that games occupy in the culture but far less into the more seminal questions of what they actually are and what pleasures they offer to attract so many millions of gamers. The closer one studies the latter set of questions, the clearer it becomes that video games operate under a different set of epistemological guidelines. They are not here to be contemplated rationally or negotiated as works of art. They do not invite the sort of subjective, distant reading that calls for Nietzsche's infinite interpretations. Instead, they facilitate the sort of emergence that is common to religious ritual, a notion that became clearer the longer I played.

As I continued to play, I became exposed to a growing number of scenarios pertinent to the game's central quest. Link, I discovered eventually, was occasionally transformed into a wolf, a mode of play that required a different subset of skills. Lupine Link moved differently from human Link—the former jumped whereas the latter dashed—and had a different set of attack moves, consisting of bites rather than sword swings, and of skills, such as howling to summon undead creatures and other animals to his aid. Still, while Lupine Link looks nothing like his human form and requires a different set of movements, I found myself needing very little time to adjust to this radical variation in the game once it first appeared. The controls, after all, were still the same, with each button representing an action belonging to the same general category; in other words, while Human Link stabbed and Lupine Link bit, two different actions, each was still achieved by pressing the same green button. The experience of play, therefore, remained consistent.

Still, trying to assess what constituted my newfound ultimate state of skill acquisition, and what differentiated it from the one directly preceding it, I noticed that the main asset I now possessed was the ability to correctly identify, analyze, and respond to a comprehensive set of situations and patterns. A video game, even one as lengthy and complex as *Twilight Princess*, just consists of code, after all, which sets an inherent limit on the size and variability of the game's world. Therefore, each video game could only contain a limited number of characters with whom the player can interact. In *The Twilight Princess*, for example, Link interacts with only sixty-five different types of characters. As each interaction, with a few exceptions, was designed to last between three and ten seconds, the game's taxonomy of combat was rather simple; each creature belonged to one of four or five subsets of enemies, and each subset could be defeated by pursuing a specific and simple technique. For example, Baris, Bombfish, and Toados, being fish or creatures that reside in water, could all be eliminated with a straightforward jab, while Big Babas, Deku Babas, and Deku Likes, all of them plants, required Link to drop a bomb into their omnivorous mouths in order to defeat them. For the sake of variety, each level was populated with at least one previously unseen pixilated meanie, as well as with combinations of creatures standing in proximity to one another and demanding that the player develop a clear and combined strategy to defeat both at the same time. Yet the aforementioned taxonomy served as a massively helpful guide; rather than spend precious moments and risk defeat trying various strategies to subdue each new creature encountered, the player needed only to briefly interact with a creature in order to call into mind the relevant combat pattern necessary to defeat it, wherein the hands retook their position at the helm. As I first encountered a Big Baba, for example, I ran to the far end of the screen; having previously interacted with Deku Babas and Deku Likes alike, both of which greatly resembled the Big Baba now in front of me, I realized that omnivorous plants required bombs. Bombs were to be obtained from Bomblings, spiderlike creatures that, when slain, left Link with a small bomb that exploded fifteen seconds after it was retrieved. And as my experience dictated that Bomblings were to be found in remote corners of the screen, that is where I headed. Defeating the Big Baba, a brand-new creature, depended on nothing but previously acquired knowledge.

The same, to be sure, is true of nearly every skill that combines cognitive and manual elements. Previous research shows an identical pattern in baseball,[38] basketball,[39] or piloting aircraft.[40] In all cases of skill acquisition, expert participants were distinguished from others of less considerable proficiency by an ability to recall at will a great number of patterns and then automatically translate the recollection into action. As psychologists Calderwood, Klein, and Crandall described that vague talent that sets a chess master apart from other players, "A central feature of a chess-master's skill is his ability to access an extensive set of recognizable chess patterns, or 'chunks.'"[41] In another study of chess players,[42] a master player was asked to compete against several other players, nearly as competent as he but not quite. As he played, the master was presented with simple math problems to solve; even though his mind was occupied by these riddles, he nonetheless succeeded in winning most of his matches. He had no need to think about his next move; his next move was immediately apparent to him, the result of having acquired the requisite level of expertise.

Still, as an expert player, I began to feel, a few hours into play at that stage, a certain degree of discomfort; having completed the game's main quest, and replaying it now strictly for my enjoyment, I was taken aback by an undercurrent of dissatisfaction. Simply stated, I was bored. My movements were now almost mechanical, my interaction with the game minimal. My body, once an excited partner, snapping along with my fingers, remained slouched on the couch. Each movement was now a repetition, each encounter a déjà vu. I played joylessly. And yet, almost instantly thereafter, I noticed a subtle but meaningful change in the schematics of my play. No longer thrilled by the challenges offered by the game, I found myself revisiting how I approached old challenges. This may seem trivial, but it startled me precisely because of its seeming negligibility: I was not seeking new ways to solve existing puzzles—which is impossible due to the nature of computer code—but rather new ways to interact with the game world's creatures, new ways of which I was, at first, unaware. For example, early on in my play I discovered that the best way to defeat a Skulltula, a spider with a skull on his back, was to jump and stab it in the center of the skull. Throughout the game I reacted thusly every time a Skulltula came into sight, leaping and stabbing. Now, however, I approached a Skulltula and cut his head off, a more difficult process that required four or five moves rather than one. I only noticed this the fourth or fifth time I met a Skulltula while in this state of ennui; watching his head fly off his body, I was jolted by the sudden realization that I'd just radically altered a pattern that I had considered, until that moment, to be inherent.

It was a surprising moment. It oughtn't to have been. As some of the most intriguing recent work on ritual suggests, such a moment of switching sensibilities is at the heart of the ritualistic experience itself. In his seminal study of the connection between ritual, religion, and politics, anthropologist Maurice Bloch described a process he named "rebounding violence," by which participants are transformed as a result of a symbolic shock that occurs during the ritual itself.

Surveying a wide array of ritualistic patterns, from those practiced in Madagascar to those observed by Japanese followers of Shinto, Bloch was surprised to discover more commonalities than the cultural and socioeconomic differences between his subjects would suggest. "The irreducible structures of religious phenomena are ritual representations of the existence of human beings in time," Bloch wrote. "In fact this ritual representation is a simple transformation of the material processes of life in plants and animals as well as humans. The transformation takes place in an idiom which has two distinguishing features."[43] At first, the ritual transports its participants from a worldly domain to a transcendental realm. "The representation of life in rituals begins with a complete inversion of everyday understandings," Bloch wrote.

> The life evoked in rituals is an "other" life, described by such words as "beyond" and "invisible," and located "in the sky," "under the earth" or "on a mountain where nobody goes." In these ritual representations, instead of birth and growth leading to a successful existence, it is weakening and death which lead to a successful existence. For example, initiation frequently begins with a symbolic "killing" of the initiates, a "killing" which negates their birth and nurturing. The social and political significance of such a passage is that by entering into a world beyond process, through the passage of reversal, one can then be part of an entity beyond process, for example, a member of a descent group. Thus, by leaving this life, it is possible to see oneself and others as part of something permanent, therefore lifetranscending.[44]

Then, Bloch continued, it is time for the ritual's participants to return to their mundane lives, yet in a way that allows them to retain the otherworldly insights they've gained during the ritual. Participants, then, reenter the world as a spaceship reenters orbit, in a violent and fiery manner, their native vitality now replaced with an external, communal one. "The return," Bloch wrote,

> is therefore a conquest of the kind of thing which had been abandoned but, as if to mark the difference between the going and the coming back, the actual identity of the vital here and now is altered. Vitality is regained, but it is not the home-grown native vitality which was discarded in the first part of the rituals that is regained, but, instead, a conquered vitality obtained from outside beings, usually animals, but sometimes plants, other peoples or women. In ritual representations, native vitality is replaced by a conquered, external, consumed vitality. It is through this substitution that an image is created in which humans can leave this life and join the transcendental, yet still not be alienated from the here and now. They become part of permanent institutions, and as superior beings they can reincorporate the present life through the idiom of conquest or consumption.[45]

An image that enables humans to leave life, join the transcendental, and yet remain connected to the here-and-now: a better definition of video games has never been offered. And it is an exceedingly radical one, impossible to understand outside the imprimatur of faith. To understand it, one need first revisit, briefly, the religious roots of all technology, and media in particular.

Scholars such as David Noble, who had surveyed the spiritual underpinnings of technology, usually tell the following story: far from rejecting science and its earthly promises, it was the monastic orders of the Middle Ages who nursed it into existence, believing that the practical arts were nothing but means to restoring humanity to its prelapsarian state. Eventually, with tools sharpened and horizons broadened, people embarked on wilder journeys; the search for Eden brought them to the New World, and the quest for technical mastery of their surroundings exponentially increased their capacity to act on their fellow humans and their natural surroundings. By the seventeenth century, to paraphrase Noble, human sights were set not so much on the Adamic but on the godly itself. Milton put it eloquently in his essay *Of Education*: We humans, he wrote, might "repair the ruins of our first parents by regaining to know God aright, and out of that knowledge to love Him, to be like Him, as we may the nearest by possessing our soul of true virtue." By the time the nineteenth century dawned, these aspirations—to be like the Divine!—were tarnished by the experience of the Industrial Revolution, which demonstrated the capacity of machines to simultaneously liberate and enslave the species. Auguste Comte, who argued that God's existence "is deeply stamped on all its creations, in morals, in the arts and sciences, in industry,"[46] nonetheless observed with trepidation the destructive power of machines. So did Karl Marx, another ambivalent soul when it came to technology. The same dichotomy grew deeper as modernity hurtled forward: from steam engines to tanks and atomic weapons and the Internet, technology gave its most astute observers ample reason to be of two minds. With each new invention, transcendence—the possibility of achieving a state of godlike command of our surroundings and erasing our all-too-human flaws—seemed imminent. With each new invention, destruction—the real possibility of Armageddon—seemed inevitable.

Nowhere, perhaps, was this construction clearer than in communications media. In his brilliant exploration of the idea of communications, John Durham Peters argued that much of the modern era has pitted Eros, that Platonic ideal of the pure and perfect communion of two minds, with the "suspicion that each of us dwells in a heart-shaped box."[47] Each of our new media—radio, television, photography, the telephone—attempted "a new kind of quasi-physical connection across the obstacles of time and space."[48] Yet they were, of course, deeply imperfect: with each new invention we learned, all the more acutely, the terms of our imperfections. The new media brought with them new specters, entities that spoke to us through time but never allowed us to speak back; "every new medium," Peters shrewdly observed, "is a machine for the production of ghosts."[49] Ours haunted us, seemingly reaffirming Socrates's suspicions when he argued, warning against the advent of writing in the *Phaedrus*, that the new medium will degrade the human mind as it would deny the readers of a text the opportunity to engage its author in dialogue.

Peters, however, warned of "the moral tyranny of the dialogue."[50] Socrates, he noted, wasn't antiquity's only communication theorist. Christ was another, and he spoke in parables, in sermons, in one-sided messages designed for an audience larger than one. Claiming a refreshing position in his scholarly field, Peters observed much of communication studies from the nineteenth century onward, keeping in line with the general ambivalence concerning technology as two-pronged, promising to bridge the chasm between individual souls on the one hand and threatening utter solipsism on the other. It's a description that holds particularly true in our time, with the Internet both boasting a staggering ability to connect people like never before and yet producing hordes of fiercely self-absorbed souls. Put bluntly, connecting to our networks, we gleefully attempt to merge with others, and when we discover the eternal limitations of humanity—the inherent shortcomings of communication that keep us at a distance even from the person standing right next to us—we rage and sink deeper into ourselves.

This bifurcated existence has produced, for the most part, flightless scholarship. The study of communication in the past three decades had largely been the study of divisions. Operating under the assumption that communion was impossible, scholars, particularly those associated with the cultural studies movement, chose to read the process of communication as a struggle between ideologically opposed groups, one long waltz of hegemony and its detractors. In such an intellectual cosmos, the individual's ability to read against the grain—see soap operas not as oppressive and misogynistic texts, say, but as rare spaces on the otherwise male-dominated airwaves for female-centric stories to unfold— was the center of attention. True to the nature of their pursuit, the cultural students both accepted the inherent impossibility of communications and swore to try and defy it, focusing on the vagaries of individual experiences that should be read simultaneously as acts of self-determination and as salvos in a larger, societal war of ideologies.

My aim here is not to criticize the field at large, merely to note that in their appetite for identity politics, many scholars have missed the great promise that digital technology—and video games first and foremost—seems to deliver, namely the ability to sidestep all of the aforementioned ontological challenges by displacing the individual subject from its central and difficult role. This is the move Maurice Bloch described so well, the move at the heart of ritual: armed with nothing but its own vitality, humanity will forever be too idiosyncratic, too unpredictable to fit in any institution. Eventually, people's desires come to odds with the common good. Ritual, Bloch argued, emptied people of these sterile desires and filled them with new, collectively sanctioned ones, instilled into them with a shock of violence—real or simulated—to the system.

My own attempts at video game phenomenology illustrate this point nicely. As I began playing I found myself simultaneously thrilled with the possibility of becoming another—Link—and frustrated by my initial inability to master the controls that would enable such unity to take place. Video games, however, being not a medium of passive observance and distant analysis but of repetitive motions, I soon overcame my trepidation. I now embodied the game. I was, to borrow Bloch's useful term, drained of my own vitality, which consisted largely of the expectation to make sense of the world as I would of a television show, and which was gratified when the game required no vigorous action but severely tested me when a foe came along and battle was called for. The game did me violence: it forced me to bend my hands and twist my fingers and strain my wrist in an effort to achieve the correct grip on the controller, and it subjected me to a stream of perpetual virtual battles, each causing me to tense my shoulders, arch my back, and furiously flick my thumbs. But the longer this violence occurred, the more ready I was to reenter the world of the game—this time, however, armed with new ways of being. I was still happy to slay and jump and perform all the necessary mundane functions of which game play consists, but, having now embodied the game's mechanical logic, I was simultaneously in it and above it. I was, as Bloch said of anyone elevated by ritual, "a changed person, a permanently transcendental person who can therefore dominate the here and now of which he previously was a part."[51]

Herein lies the major difference between video games and other media. Gamers, as I argue in the following chapters, see themselves and their interactions with the medium in terms of communion and, to a lesser extent, community. Trained to obey the stringent dictates of a preordained digital realm, they regain agency by first abandoning it and then forging it anew after hours of struggling to achieve maximum grip. Such a process considerably weakens their subjective selves, but it awards them in return with a kind of unified experience that television or radio could never give them, namely the resolution of the constant tension

urging them to connect with others and simultaneously reminding them that such connection is impossible. To explore this state
of being at greater length, it is worthwhile to observe gamers not
at their best behavior but at their most questionable, as they toss
away the rules and cheat.

3

The Sweet Cheat

THE UTILITY AND THE ECSTASY OF BREAKING THE RULES

One recent evening I had the opportunity to observe the young son of good friends play a new video game. Before he'd even ripped open the packaging, the boy darted to his room, returning a few minutes later with a piece of paper on which he'd sloppily scribbled a set of markings. Then he popped the game into his Xbox, peeked at the rumpled sheet in his hand, and started tapping buttons on his controller in rapid sequence. He was entering cheat codes, and soon their effects were evident on screen: the boy's avatar now had endless ammunition, bigger guns, invincibility, invisibility, immortality. He floated through the game like a punishing god, smiting. Through all this, the little boy giggled. I asked him if he was playing fair, and he said no. I asked if he was ashamed; a little, he replied. I asked if he ever played without cheat codes. This made him laugh. "No way!" he said, and went back to the game.

And then it hit me: the kid was Faust. Bored and desiring infinite knowledge, he didn't even have to wait for his Mephistopheles to knock. Nowadays, there's an abundance of devils on the Internet eagerly anticipating people interested in selling their soul. I've been in the habit of thinking about both video games and religion for a long stretch, some of it professionally, but the observation left me in a grim mood. The abundance of video game cheating, I mused, said nothing good about the world as a drama of salvation.

In fact, the whole scene itself seemed like a cheat: after millennia of slowly and carefully nudging humanity closer to a prelapsarian state of mastery over the world and all its natural phenomena, technology seemed to have finally slipped into its metaphase. Instead of providing us the knowledge and the tools to remake our world, it now produced carefully manicured alternate realities, little miniature universes for us to toy with, complete with a list of cheats to make us feel almighty. It was an oppressive proposition: Did the abundance of cheating mean that video games were truly the escapist, numbing, callous medium their critics have always accused them of being? A further investigation is in order.

It begins, as always, with history. The first recorded cheat in the history of electronic games dates back to 1983, with the game *Manic Miner*. Writing about the game a year after its publication, *Your Spectrum*, one of the first magazines for PC users (in this case, owners of the early brand Sinclair Spectrum), noted the innovation of cheating:

> To finish up, let's take a look at the one that started it
> all off—*Manic Miner*. Although it's getting on a bit now,
> there's still a few people out there who don't know the
> "easy" way of moving about the rooms. On the original
> Bug-Byte version, you have to type in the sequence of
> numbers "6031769" (reputed to be Matthew Smith's old
> phone number) and, while holding down the "6" key
> press combinations of keys "1" to "5" to move around.[1]

Installed by Smith, the game's designer and programmer, the cheat, awarding the player unlimited lives, was created in order to allow for easier play testing. As electronic games began to move away from the single-screen days of *Pac-Man* or *Space Invaders*, game designers faced increasingly complex, rolling narratives that featured several screens and required careful attention to issues of continuity and playability. To ensure that the game "made sense," namely that the play experience was uninterrupted by any inherent flaw in the design, designers began installing codes to help themselves quickly play through games and check their consistency, avoiding the cumbersome and time-consuming process of playing by the game's rules. What constituted the essence of the game for players, then—its challenges and temporary setbacks—was, from a designer's point of view, an irksome delay.

Play tests were intended to examine flow and little else, and therefore means of eradicating the limitations set on an ordinary player—primarily running out of "lives," or turns—were necessary. Finding even unlimited "lives" insufficient, Smith installed an additional cheat, this one allowing the player to shift between each of the game's screens, called caverns, by holding down different combinations of numbers on the keyboard. Faithful to the recognition that games are code, Smith's cheat allowed the player to pick a cavern based on a combination corresponding to its binary number; the first cavern, for example, called the Central Cavern, could be accessed by holding down 6 (here representing zero), while the next screen, called the Cold Room, could be accessed by holding down 6 and 1, represented on the screen as 00001.[2]

Despite the game's popularity, however, its cheats never became widely known, and they were reserved for players who possessed the technical ability to peek at the game's code. All that, however, changed a year later, when the sequel to *Manic Miner* made cheating a necessity. Following the success of his debut title, Smith decided to create another game that would focus on the same character, a miner named Willy. That game was titled *Jet Set Willy* and depicted its protagonist, now wealthy due to his exploits in the first game, running around his newly purchased mansion and battling strange demons abandoned there by the previous tenant. The game was an instant hit with users,[3] due mainly to its excellent graphics, innovative items (Willy interacted with such novelties as swinging ropes, moving blades, and a coterie of strange, funny animals), and most importantly, its groundbreaking design. Unlike the classic side-scrollers of the time, *Jet Set Willy* allowed players to explore Willy's house on their own terms, moving back and forth from screen to screen as they pleased, the first video game to allow such freedom of movement.

Successful as it was, *Jet Set Willy* suffered from one fatal flaw. As the player entered a room called the Attic, an error in the path of an arrow, or a piece of code, would occur, resulting in the game's memory being overtaxed and leading to the overriding of crucial game elements. Monsters would disappear, items would be misplaced, and worst of all, subsequent entries into other rooms, after visiting the Attic, would lead to instant death. Alarmed by the flaws, the game's publisher, Software Projects, first claimed that the discrepancies were an intentional feature aimed at making the game more difficult, even going so far as to claim a narrative-based reasoning for the sudden-death scenario: the rooms in question, they claimed, were filled with poisonous gas.[4] Soon thereafter, however, the company realized the extent of its problem and offered a reward to whomever succeeded in beating the game: a bottle of champagne and a helicopter ride in London's skies, piloted by the company's CEO.[5] Two players, Ross Holman and Cameron Else, eventually succeeded in the task, doing so with the help of PEEKs, a function in the BASIC computer programming language designed to read the contents of memory cells at a specified address, and POKEs, a corresponding command that sets the contents of such cells. In other words, Holman and Else ended up rewriting the game's code, de facto correcting the flaws in Software Projects' original design. The company eventually published four of Holman and Else's POKEs, including the one that enabled players to overcome the bug in the Attic.[6] Players, then, were not only encouraged to cheat, but armed with the knowledge, however limited, to rewrite code.[7]

Jet Set Willy launched a deluge of interest in code writing among gamers. Given BASIC's prominence as a programming language, and given its relative simplicity—based, as it was, on storing numerical values in memory—and its linear form, even users with a limited understanding of computer science could access the menu before running the game, alter a few lines, and then play a largely modified version of their own making. In the classic *Heroquest*, for example, anyone wishing to alter the protagonist's speed—the inconsistency of which was a major difficulty for players—needed only to enter the following code:

```
10 REM GNOMISH HEROQUEST HACK
20 CLEAR 24575
30 LOAD ""CODE 16384: LOAD"" CODE
40 POKE 34151, 182
50 LET MC=USR 28030[8]
```

The first line notifies the computer of the intended destination, in this case the game *Heroquest*; the second and third lines direct toward a specific component of the game, namely the speed at which the hero moves; the crucial fourth line inserts the POKE, essentially rewriting the game's code by altering the relevant memory cells; and the fifth line implements the command and weaves it into the rest of the code. This, in my opinion, is the closest that video games have ever been to true interactivity; given that their nature, their essence, is code, enabling players to alter the code at will, each according to a player's own whim, made for a collaborative, highly personalized product. While a majority of cheats focused either on fixing bugs in the original program or on altering elements that made play too difficult or repetitive, some—such as changing the color pattern, for example—were simply flourishes.[9]

Such freedom, however, carried with it a few distinct disadvantages for game designers and publishers. First and foremost was the threat of piracy. Games that could be easily "cracked" could also be easily copied. The industry at the time, lacking a powerful digital distribution platform such as the Internet, relied heavily on what Gary McGraw and Greg Hoglund called the "over-the-counter paradigm,"[10] namely selling individually packaged units at various retail stores. A cracked game could spell the end of the profit stream for a specific title. As Hoglund and McGraw noted, "Game makers have justifiably gone to great lengths to thwart [game cracking]. . . . In the end, the games were always cracked—but in some cases, the countermeasures delayed the release of a cracked version by days or even weeks. This delay earned real revenue for the game companies, because delaying a crack for even a week translated into hundreds of thousands of dollars in sales."[11]

Cheating eventually brought about a flurry of legal action, chief among them the previously discussed case of Midway versus those *Pac-Man* imitators, Artic; with Artic's stinging defeat, few companies attempted similar brazen knockoffs. Technology, however, soon created new opportunities for messing with code. As arcade consoles gave way to PCs, cheating was once again a prevalent issue, although the legal challenge was more difficult for game publishers, who now had to battle not copycat manufacturers but a multitude of users who, given the nature of the personal computer, now had access to the source. As McGraw and Hoglund noted, game publishers spent the early 1980s devising all manners of countermeasures preventing users from accessing their codes.[12] By the late 1980s and early 1990s, however, the market for electronic games was almost entirely dominated not by PCs but by the newest new technology, home consoles, from the early Atari 2600 to the later, and immensely popular, Nintendo Entertainment System (NES). On the surface, the move from PC to console appeared to render cheating obsolete. Unlike a PC, which allowed access to the software's code, the new consoles were, quite literally, closed systems, encased in wood or plastic and largely tamper-proof. To rewire an NES, basic knowledge of programming and a touch of common sense were no longer sufficient. One needed tools, components, and a keen understanding of the principles of electrical engineering.

But the freedom players experienced in the heady days of the PC was hard to relinquish. By the arrival of the NES in the United States in 1985, code writing had become a popular pastime for players, with magazines such as *CRASH*—enjoying, by 1986, a circulation of upward of 100,000 readers[13]—regularly publishing lists of POKE commands for various games. It was only natural, then, that when the NES became a phenomenon (Nintendo claims to have sold more than 60 million units worldwide),[14] third-party companies would rise to try and restore to video game consoles the freedom associated with the PC. This, at first, appeared particularly feasible, as both early PCs and the NES were 8-bit machines, meaning that their memory addresses were at most one octet wide. Given the similarities between consoles and PCs, a solution was sought to overcome the fact that the NES had no keyboard, ran no accessible operating system, and allowed the player limited interaction besides inserting cartridges and playing specific games. The NES also came equipped with the 10NES, an authentication system consisting of a computer chip that would check the cartridge inserted into the NES for authentication, and a chip in the cartridge that would provide the 10NES code upon demand. If the cartridge did not provide the required code, the system would not boot up. Nintendo registered the 10NES under US Patent 4,799,635, and the source code was copyrighted, allowing only Nintendo the authority to produce authorization chips.

The best way to override the 10NES, hackers and manufacturers soon realized, was by installing a dongle, or an add-on cartridge that attaches itself to a legitimate game cartridge, uses its authorization code, and then overrides its content. As such equipment was costly and complicated to manufacture, it fell to professional developers, in this case British game publishers Codemasters, to create a dongle that could be sold for home use. The result, released in 1991, was the Game Genie, distributed in the United States by Lewis Galoob Toys Inc., a cartridge that allowed players to insert codes into the NES, and later into the Super NES and a few other consoles as well. Given the lack of access to the game's actual source code, the Game Genie, having overridden the 10NES protection measures, directed players to a screen where they could feed the machine codes painstakingly discovered by professional hackers. With the entire program no longer visible, such a method was, at best, inefficient; as the company's own (archived) website admits,[15] many games on many consoles remained untouchable to the Game Genie, and even those whose codes were cracked could quite easily introduce an upgraded version with revamped code. As this was the case, the Game Genie often ended up entering obsolete or incorrect codes, leading the console to freeze and gaining a reputation for precariousness.

But the Game Genie was to leave an indelible mark, not in the marketplace, but in the courtroom. Almost immediately after the product hit the market, Nintendo of America sued Lewis Galoob. As Nintendo's business model relied heavily on charging game developers exorbitant fees for licensing deals—Nintendo would manufacture the game cartridges itself, requiring game publishers to order large quantities in advance, so that even a game that was a commercial flop would still be profitable for Nintendo—the possibility of overriding the 10NES authentication system meant that the Game Genie, besides utilizing cheats in legitimate Nintendo games, could also allow the console to play nonofficial games, and such games began to appear on the market soon after the Game Genie was introduced. As nonofficial games were a major financial loss for Nintendo, the company, already litigious, was particularly concerned with a courtroom victory. As the clearest precedent for the case, *Midway v. Arctic*, was decided in favor of the plaintiff, Nintendo was optimistic, suing Galoob for copyright infringement and claiming that the Game Genie consisted of a derivative work, violating Nintendo's copyright to its own video game. On this basis, Nintendo asked for a preliminary injunction. The court, however, refused to oblige; the Game Genie, it ruled, did not create a derivative work. Furthermore, even if it did, such work might well fall under the banner of fair use. "Having paid Nintendo a fair return," read the court's opinion, "the consumer may experiment with the product and create new variations of play, for personal enjoyment, without creating a derivative work."[16]

The Galoob case, still considered a primer in assessing users' rights to interact with new technologies,[17] sent ripples throughout the gaming industry.[18] The Game Genie itself died a quiet death by its own hand; not having access to the source code, and having to resort to entering cheat codes at random, the cartridge proved to be of limited appeal to players. And while no successor attempted to produce a similar device—again, mainly due to technical limitations—console manufacturers nonetheless realized the existence of a hunger for cheating. It was a desire that they didn't wholly understand but would be foolish to ignore.

Remarkably, Nintendo took the first step. As early as 1987, and up to the Galoob case, Nintendo released a series of annual strategy guides, designed as supplements to its official magazine, *Nintendo Power*. Each numbering several dozen pages, the guides were distributed only to the magazine's subscribers, numbering roughly 1.2 million by 1991.[19] While not technically strategy guides, the four issues included several pages of walkthroughs, as well as a few tips on how to beat the most difficult enemies at each level of the approximately three dozen games reviewed in each guide. They did not, however, offer comprehensive, step-by-step accounts of how to beat the game; offered no cheat codes; and devoted a considerable amount of space to further discussing the games' backstory, characters, and other issues secondary to the game play itself. Most of the emphasis, in other words, was on what Katie Salen and Eric Zimmerman defined as "beyond-the-object interactivity,"[20] namely an approach by game designers to convince players to commit to the game by creating a strong culture surrounding the game that would then affect and enhance the play experience itself.

After Galoob, however, the company took a step in a different direction. Rather than naming its guide, as it had done before, simply "Official Nintendo Player's Guide," the 1992 volume was titled "Top Secret Passwords" and featured not only detailed walkthroughs but also passwords and, for the first time, cheat codes (namely, sequences of actions a player could perform on-screen and unlock secret powers or discover hidden objects) for selected games. Accordingly, Nintendo's fan club, admission to which was automatic for the magazine's subscribers, was now renamed the Super Power Club. Shortly thereafter, *Nintendo Power* itself began to undergo an editorial shift, with three significant permanent features added:

> **Beat the Boss**: Detailed information on how to beat one or more "boss" enemies in a specific game, often including cheat codes.
> **Counselors' Corner**: Nintendo employees responding to readers' game-related questions. The questions almost always pertained to strategy, and the responses almost always included a cheat or two.
> **NES Achievers / Power Player's Challenge**: An ongoing roster of high scores submitted by players, with top performers winning such prizes as T-shirts, key-chains, and so on.

Nintendo was beginning to institutionalize cheating by offering cheats and codes in its own magazine and initiating contests to enhance players' sense of competition. However, the "authentic" representatives of fan culture—namely, those publications and organizations unaffiliated with console manufacturers or game publishers that were established in order to serve as an independent voice for the gaming community—were moving in the opposite direction, chastising the practice of cheating and focusing on beyond-the-object interactivity, backstories, fan culture, and so forth. The best example of such behavior is *Amiga Power*, an independent magazine for users of the then-popular Amiga personal computer that focused solely on gaming. Publishing its first issue in May 1991, *Amiga Power* enjoyed a limited run of five years, mainly due to the magazine's fierce adherence to editorial independence; unlike the majority of game magazines at the time, *Amiga Power* did not succumb to game publishers' demands and was often punished by loss of advertising revenue or withdrawal of advanced review copies of games. And while *Amiga Power* still enjoyed a modicum of popularity—the magazine's circulation, an average of 55,000 copies per month,[21] was a medium-high figure for an independent magazine of its sort at the time—it was unable to offer its subscribers any of the increasingly tempting perks, such as discounts on future games, that the magazines published by Nintendo and other game companies regularly featured. Despite its clout among gamers at the time, *Amiga Power* shut down after publishing only sixty-five issues.

Reading about these issues in retrospect, two things stand out. First of all, *Amiga Power* strongly endorsed the idea that all players should interact with games by engaging themselves in a beyond-the-game reimagining of the game's culture. For example, the magazine had a recurring feature titled "In the Style Of," which encouraged readers to send in depictions of game characters, drawn in the style of other game characters (a fierce robotic soldier from one popular game, say, drawn with the soft, pastel-based palette of another game); it also ran many game reviews that poked fun at the conventions of certain game genres and featured occasional fictitious interviews with game characters, written without the permission or cooperation of the game's designers or publishers.

Another recurrent feature was the magazine's continued commitment to "fairness," from both the designers' and the players' end. *Amiga Power* featured a regular installment titled "Kangaroo Court," in which designers were chided for creating elements of a game that were unfair to players, such as rooms that instantly killed any character who entered them, unexplained and illogical traps or hidden doors, or any other behavior that spoiled the player's experience. Contesting the then-popular design convention of joystick-reversing powerups, for example—in which a certain item, obtained by the unwitting player, reverses the game's control systems (up becoming down, etc.)—writer Jonathan Davies struck an angry note: "I mean, why not go the whole hog and have something that disables the controls altogether, or makes the screen go completely blank, or punches you in the face, pees in your beer and steals your girlfriend?"[22]

Even more vociferous, however, was the magazine's disdain for players who utilized cheat codes. *Amiga Power* constantly published remarks discouraging its readers from cheating, often calling those who did offensive names. The magazine's forty-seventh issue, for example, published in March 1995, featured a page-three advertisement touting the current issue's contents. It read, "We expose the FEEBLE-MINDED IMPOTENCE of those who cheat." The story itself, titled "Scum," consisted mainly of strongly worded insults directed at anyone in the habit of cheating in video games.

Finally, to undermine the increasingly competitive attitude among players—an attitude promoted heavily by *Nintendo Power* and the other magazines published by console manufacturers and game publishers, which promised players tangible rewards as well as mentions in print for breaking game records—*Amiga Power* initiated its own series of contests, focusing not on proficiency of play but rather on zany, imaginative ideas. One contest, for example, urged the readers to design a ludicrous spy trap befitting the most far-fetched of James Bond films, while another had readers imagine what an ultimate video game villain would look like. The contests, in other words, were more creative than competitive, and they had little to do with the games themselves.

The differences between *Nintendo Power* and *Amiga Power* are striking. The independent, player-oriented magazine took a distinct stance against cheating (even the publication's "Letters to the Editor" section was given the punning title "Do the Write Thing"), promoted fairness, devoted many pages to game culture, and shunned competitiveness. The corporate publication not only endorsed competitiveness—an understandable stance—but also depended on cheating as a major marketing strategy, luring players with sanctioned cheat codes that helped them overcome the challenges presented by the very games that constituted the core of Nintendo's earnings.

At first glance, such an approach seems, at best, counterintuitive. If games are at the heart of Nintendo's operations, and if games, according to our common understanding, involve the voluntary acceptance of an agreed-upon, solid set of rules, why would cheating or subverting these rules be permitted? The answer has to do with the designers' increasing realization that far from mere digressions or transgressions, cheat codes can be used as important design tools solving what is perhaps the key existential conundrum of video games—namely, manufacturing the illusion of choice in an algorithmic environment that offers a rigidly constructed script and eliminates chance.

To examine this claim, consider first one key element of play, that of tension, as defined by Johan Huizinga:

> Tension means uncertainty, chanciness; a striving to decide the issue and so end it. The player wants something

> to "go," to "come off"; he wants to "succeed" by his own
> exertions. Baby reaching for a toy, pussy patting a bobbin,
> a little girl playing ball—all want to achieve something
> difficult, to succeed, to end a tension. Play is "tense," as we
> say. It is this element of tension and solution that governs
> all solitary games of skill and application such as puzzles,
> jig-saws, mosaic-making, patience, target-shooting, and
> the more play bears the character of competition the
> more fervent it will be.[23]

Tension is at the core of the play instinct. Eager to restore order
and eliminate uncertainty—uncertainty that is the opening condition and the driving force of any game—the player must be curbed
in by a counterforce that ensures that all those engaged in the
game enjoy equal access to its framework. That same force must
also guarantee that the player who emerges victorious does so
solely on the basis of some combination, in varying ratios, of skill
and luck. That force is referred to simply as "the rules."

In games previously characterized as games of emergence, such
a force is paramount. Imagine, for example, a football game in
which the players of one team stepped onto the field armed with
clubs, which they would then proceed to use every time their
opponents tried to tackle. Such a move, it is easy to imagine, would
not only constitute a blatant infringement of the game's rules but
would also arouse deep resentment in most spectators. Once the
clubs were introduced, most people would claim that the game
played on the field could no longer be referred to as "football," as
it blatantly violated the rules around which football as a game is
constructed, that is to say, the very essence of football. Such is the
case with all games of emergence; built as they are around a prescribed system of closely set rules, the games unfold in accordance
with these rules, based, once more, on skill and luck. Football,
for example, has a few dozen rules that govern each encounter

between two teams of players. Every game of football, therefore, is a variation on a theme. The rules of football allow only so many maneuvers, and the specific maneuvers applied throughout the course of a specific game depend on the athleticism, competence, and preparedness of the players—in short, their skill—as well as on luck; a pass missed by an inch or two, for example, could change the course of the game. The rules, then, are important not only to safeguard fair play and ensure—to use an appropriate sports cliché—an even playing field, but because, in a sense, they *are* the game. If games of emergence, as I have previously demonstrated, consist of a small number of strict rules that, in turn, generate a wide array of scenarios, then altering the rules alters the very DNA of the game itself.

Such, however, is not the case with games of progression. Video games, currently the sole type of game in this nascent category, are written not from beginning to end—namely, prescribed rules dictating a large number of possible outcomes—but from end to beginning, with a strict linear narrative dictating specific movements and sequences at each turn of the game. That being the case, games of progression differ from games of emergence in several notable ways.

The first key difference has to do with the termination of luck. Quite literally, luck plays no part in video games, as it is antithetical to their very building blocks: lines of code. To better understand this, I examine one popular algorithm frequently used in video game design and its relationship to chance. The algorithm, known as "a star" and represented as A*, is the most popular choice applied by programmers when tackling the issue of pathfinding. As each video game takes place in a virtual environment, represented graphically as a grid, programmers need to create elegant solutions to allow for movement around the grid, avoiding obstacles and expending a minimal amount of energy.

Traditionally, the problem of pathfinding has had two distinct solutions. The first, known as Dijkstra's algorithm, begins with a definitive starting point and then repeatedly examines the closest path to the destination, expanding outward until the goal is finally reached. While the algorithm is guaranteed to find the shortest path to the goal, its method of selecting the point of origin as its departure and then scanning all paths close to it makes it a relatively time-consuming computation. To speed up the action, another algorithm was created, known as the Best-First-Search (BFS) algorithm. The major difference here is that BFS has an estimate, or a heuristic, of how far from the goal any given object may be, and then works backward from the goal itself to the starting point. The heuristic guarantees a significantly shorter computation, but, given its nature—rather than a single if-then construct, it allows for several such options in a complicated tree of probabilities—is not guaranteed to find a shorter path. In 1968 A* was introduced to combine the two algorithms into one, looking both at the starting point and the goal. As computer programmer Amit Patel explains it:

> In the standard terminology used when talking about A*, $g(n)$ represents the cost of the path from the starting point to any vertex n, and $h(n)$ represents the heuristic estimated cost from vertex n to the goal. . . . A* balances the two as it moves from the starting point to the goal. Each time through the main loop, it examines the vertex n that has the lowest $f(n) = g(n) + h(n)$.[24]

Even without delving into the intricacies of the algorithm, it is apparent that A* leaves no room for chance. People seeking the shortest path around an obstacle in a nonvirtual environment might change their minds according to a variety of factors, from concrete conditions such as visibility on the field (which might change according to the weather or the time of day) to ephemeral ones such as mood. As a result, a person might perform a certain action one time and another the next. The same person, however, playing a video game is merely interacting with an algorithm, and an algorithm always generates either the exact same or one of a very small batch of actions, the consequences of which are always identical. This is true even in the case of advanced heuristics; even the most diverse computational tree, one that allows the algorithms to take into consideration many conditions, still operates within a strictly confined environment in which possibilities are limited and each action always brings about the same outcome. For this reason, constructs of artificial intelligence—a notion often based on complex heuristics—are exceedingly competent at such activities as chess, which depend solely on computing a vast quantity of possibilities at each turn and finding an optimal solution, but not, say, at conversation. Any amount of speech data fed into the machine could not prepare it for the wonderful randomness that so often dominates human interaction, one that could carry a conversation from nuclear proliferation to the latest celebrity foible in a moment, often based not on clear causality but on free association, whim, or happenstance.

The games humans play are rife with chance, as we ourselves are subject to so many incomputable factors such as emotion, environment, and our perception of others. None of these factors, however, are represented in video games. The algorithm dictates that each time a player presses a button the character on screen jumps in the air and lands on its feet. It always jumps to the same exact height and always lands perfectly. Nothing could go wrong with its actions, with the sole exception of the player missing the cue and pressing the button too early or too late. If that is the case, the algorithm does nothing but simply repeat itself, giving the player the opportunity to repeat the same action again, until getting it just right.

Luck, therefore, is eliminated, and with it tension in Huizinga's sense. While game play, when in progress, can be a rather tense experience, the repetitive nature of algorithms and the fact that any failed action could be redone immediately thereafter eliminate any concrete tension from the outset. Unlike, say, a football match, there is no chance of loss; playing a game of video game football, the player need only press the button anew to activate the game once more and try again until victory is achieved. And unlike in Monopoly or blackjack, for example, there is no danger of drawing unpropitious cards or anticipation of drawing beneficial ones; the same exact patterns recur each and every time, the same enemies appear, and the same exact sequence helps defeat them. With the elimination of concrete tension, the rules themselves are no longer necessary as a safeguard.

Unlike games of emergence, where the rules serve as a sequence generator of sorts, in games of progression there can only be one possible scenario, with the player's goal being the playing out of that scenario while learning how to navigate the closed system that is the game's world. The rules, then, are best thought of not as independent parameters but rather as tools that help the player adjust to the designer's grand vision. And since the player can only do what the code has carefully defined, nothing lies outside the realm of the rules, and therefore no distinction exists between obedience and deviance from a rule-based standpoint. Put simply, if the purpose of video game play is to adhere to the designer's narrative, and if code disallows taking any measure that was not previously made possible by the designer, then nothing the player does can actually be said to constitute cheating. Seen from the player's perspective, this basic notion regarding the nature of video games was perfectly expressed by one player I interviewed: if the game allows it, it isn't cheating.

What, then, is it? To answer the question, it helps to consider a well-known game-related scandal not often thought of as an instance of cheating. In 2004, Rockstar, a video game publisher, released *Grand Theft Auto: San Andreas*, the latest installment in the popular series of fast-paced games. One of the innovations of the game over the giddy, wanton violence of its predecessors was the ability of the main character, a thug named Carl "CJ" Johnson, to date up to six women, going on missions to retrieve specific objects in order to improve his chances with a specific potential paramour. Once Johnson retrieves all the objects, the respective date asks him to follow her into her house for "hot coffee"; the camera remains outside the house, but loud, obscene noises suggesting copulation are heard in the soundtrack. In 2005, when the game was released for personal computers (the initial release, as is the case with most *Grand Theft Auto* games, was for Sony's Playstation 2 alone), a mod—or a hacked bit of code that modifies the game's original course—appeared, called the "hot coffee mod." Created by a thirty-seven-year-old Dutch hacker named Patrick Wildenborg, the mod allowed the player to actually enter the house with Johnson and control his actions during the animated copulation sequence.

The mod was posted on several websites and was soon discovered by the game's community of dedicated fans. It didn't take long for "Hot Coffee" to become widespread, and, as could be expected, the mod sparked the fury of many. It prompted, for example, Senator Hillary Clinton to introduce a federally mandated enforcement of a ratings system for video games and moved the city of Los Angeles to file a lawsuit against the game's publishers, accusing it of failure to disclose the game's sexual content. No one, however, was more indignant than the publishers themselves. The mod, they claimed, violated the game's End User License Agreement and was the work of hackers who had applied complex technological tools to crack the game. "Since the 'Hot Coffee' scenes cannot be created without intentional and significant technical modifications and reverse-engineering of the game's source code," read the company's statement, "we are currently investigating ways that we can increase the security protection of the source code and prevent the game from being altered by the 'Hot Coffee' modification."[25]

Shortly after the statement was released, however, discussions on Internet forums began demonstrating that the controversial content, while unlocked by the mod, was nonetheless built into not only the PC version but also into the console version as well, meaning that it had to have been programmed in advance by Rockstar's designers themselves. Wildenborg claimed that, far from requiring great technical know-how, his mod only changed one bit in the game, the "main.scm" file, creating absolutely no new content.[26] Moreover, further scrutiny by game enthusiasts online showed that some of the animation used in the sexually themed minigames appeared in the unmodified game itself, clearly visible in the background. This was the case even after Rockstar released a modified version of the game a few months later. In his blog, game designer and critic Michael Russell explained the inclusion, saying that built-in hidden sequences necessarily use both the game's engine and art, and therefore cannot simply be removed; furthermore, he added, such games were considered by designers to be a way to attract—and reward—committed gamers, giving them an additional challenge cloaked by an air of mystery.[27]

While the "hot coffee" minigame may not appear to be a cheat per se—the player, after all, does not advance in any way by unlocking these veiled sequences—it nonetheless reflects the logic of game designers vis-à-vis cheats. Theoretically, as per Rockstar's original statement, any mods should be discouraged by publishers, as they violate the End User License Agreement and put the publisher at risk of suffering public calumny should a creative hacker come up with particularly offensive content. Yet, not only has Rockstar left its code open for players to present mods to personalize their game (creating, for example, better cars for their characters, or nicer clothes), but it has also, as the "hot coffee" saga demonstrated, actively planted mods into its own game. And while the player does not gain invincibility or ammunition by applying the necessary mod and playing out the pornographic scenes, the player nonetheless enjoys an advantage over other players who haven't done so. The scene, in other words, was a reward, planted in the game for the most dedicated players to toil and find.

While no concrete figures exist regarding the number of games that utilize any sort of designer-sanctioned cheat—consisting, in this case, of anything from minigames to invincibility codes—surveying the top-selling games for the various editions of consoles by Nintendo, Sega, Sony, and Microsoft[28] and then consulting with websites and guides devoted to cheats reveals that an overwhelming majority of the most popular games of the last two decades contain some element of designer-sanctioned cheat in them, from the rather benign cheats that unlock nothing more crucial than an alternative credit sequence to the more concrete cheats that give the player advantages that help with more rapid advancement.

At first glance, this may seem baffling. Given the previous discussion concerning the nature of video game design, a logical expectation, given the primacy of the principle of intention, is never to present the player with any obstacles or challenges the solutions for which are not readily comprehensible. If successful play, after all, revolves around the player devising and implementing plans that help navigate the closed-system laid down by the designer, the insertion of an unknowable sequence appears to be detrimental. Why, then, do designers insert cheats of various forms into games?

The subject remains largely untouched. Of the two dozen designers interviewed for this book, none felt inclined to address the topic, either belittling it—in the words of one designer, as "something we do for fun"—or denying its prevalence altogether. A similar review of design literature—from books to websites—showed virtually no mention of cheats, codes, and so on. Cheating, then, is the bête noire of video game design: it is ever there, its faint growl audible, and yet nearly no one is prepared to address its existence or discuss its nature. Throughout the course of my interviews and literature review pertaining to this topic, however, an explanation did begin to emerge: cheating, properly considered, is nothing if not an abstract design tool for creating intention, or the players' ability to make an implementable plan of their own that emanates from their understanding of the game's options. In this setting, cheating emerges as an illusion of transgression that imbues the play with new, thrilling meaning. Perhaps Nintendo realized this instinctively after the Galoob case, and the reason it changed its publication's name to convey a mock-insider feeling, as if to say, "We who are in the know, know how to cheat; and we who cheat are in the know."

Raphael "Raph" Koster, one of the leading game designers working today and the creative force behind such hits as the *Ultima Online* and *Star Wars Galaxies* series, sees the application of cheats as a crucial element in game design. In his book, *Theory of Fun for Game Design*, Koster writes:

> Once a player looks at a game and ascertains the pattern and the ultimate goal, they'll try to find the optimal path to getting there. And one of the classic problems with games of all sorts is that players often have little compunction about violating the theoretical "magic circle" that encompasses games and makes them protected spaces in which to practice.
>
> In other words, many players are willing to cheat.
>
> This is a natural impulse. It's not a sign of people being bad (though we can call it bad sportsmanship). It's actually a sign of lateral thinking, which is a very important and valuable mental skill to learn. When someone cheats at a game, they may be acting unethical, but they're also exercising a skill that makes them more likely to survive. It's often called "cunning." . . .

> When a player cheats in a game, they are choos-
> ing a battlefield that is broader in context than the
> game itself. Cheating is a sign that the player is in fact
> grokking the game.[29]

Koster's choice of words in the last paragraph suggests a more nuanced understanding of game design, offering, as it does, a startling solution to the apparent tension between the notion of intention and the abundance of sanctioned cheating. The key term he uses is "grokking," coined in 1961 by science fiction writer Robert A. Heinlein in his novel *Stranger in a Strange Land*. Defined in its transitive sense by the *Oxford English Dictionary*, the term means "to understand intuitively or by empathy; to establish rapport with," and in the intransitive sense as "to empathize or communicate sympathetically with; also, to experience enjoyment." Heinlein's own usage of it was even more forceful; a staple of the Martian language spoken throughout the book, it literally means "to drink," while the essential meaning is to grasp the essence of something to such a degree that it becomes part of one and one becomes part of it.

Koster is de facto suggesting that one way to grok a game is to prove that one sees through it. As Koster notes, players have little compunction about violating the "magic circle" in which games unfold safely and according to a rigidly observed system of rules. Games we truly love cannot be contained by circles, magical or otherwise, and have a way of becoming our entire world. To serve us well, game designers ought to recognize this condition and allow us if not an actual cheat—that would require rewriting code—then the illusion thereof.

Interviews with gamers and game designers alike suggest that this approach is prevalent. One former middle-level designer working for a large studio defined cheating in terms similar Koster's. "We install cheats into the game because they're fun," he said.

Think back to when we were kids; which is more fun, winning anything the hard way, or pulling off some stunt that proves you to be so powerful, you're not even playing the same game as other people anymore? This is why we like superheroes. They're super. They're not just winning against crime, winning against the bad guys, by playing by the rules. The police play by the rules, and they could never stop [Superman's archnemesis] Lex Luthor. But Superman can. How? By cheating. He can fly. That's not fair. Lex Luthor can't fly. The police can't fly. Superman is cheating, because he is, literally, a super-man. So Luthor cheats by finding Kryptonite, which is the only thing Superman can't handle. None of them play by the rules, but we don't care. We just want to see the good guy win. . . . It's a bit like wrestling: We know it's fake, and all we care about is the good guy, our guy, coming out on top.[30]

The point of the game, he added, was to establish mastery, not to play fair. "You play to win," he said. "Why else would you play?" When asked what, if anything, was the role of enjoyment in play, the designer replied that while enjoyment, or fun, was obviously an important factor, "You can't separate the fun from winning, at least not anymore. The games nowadays are all about winning, and so many of them don't even let you play half the game unless you win the other half first." He gave as an example a game he himself participated in designing, in which a wide range of missions, weapons, and vehicles were only available once the player had completed numerous missions of ascending complexity, not an uncommon trend in contemporary game design. "So," he added, "the game sends you this message that to have fun, you have to win. . . . Winning becomes the game, and you do whatever you take to get to that point."[31]

The desire to win, of course, is a crucial component of every instance of game play in general. A poker player, say, might find it difficult to enjoy the game if each hand lost money. But a game of poker is a space of possibilities defined equally by skill—the ability to keep a straight face, maybe—and luck—the cards one draws. Video games, on the other hand, demand a modicum of skill, but, as previously discussed, have eliminated luck; one always meets the same challenges in the same sequence each time one plays. Therefore, winning is the only way a player has of experiencing the game in its entirety—gamers play to beat the game, and cheats help them achieve this goal.

In-depth interviews with gamers seemed to affirm this notion. MI, for example, a twenty-five-year-old New Yorker who is a self-described hardcore gamer, admitted to seldom interacting with a game without downloading a significant number of cheats and codes first. Most recently, he said, he had bought a game in which the player must survive a zombie attack while trapped in a local mall; before beginning to play, MI said, he had surfed cheat websites and found a code that allowed him infinite ammunition and considerably augmented energy. "I wanted to see what the game had to offer," he said, "and to do that you have to have cheats." Engaging with the game to its fullest capacity, he said—doing anything from completing its main quest to unraveling hidden minigames—was, to him, the sole point of playing the game. An underutilized game, he said, is "like buying a DVD of a movie you can only watch a third of the way through. What I hate the most is these games that don't let you do anything unless you spend hours leveling up. What's the point? If the game has stuff to offer, I want to see it all"—and, he replied when asked, whenever possible, all at once.

Yet even when the overwhelming majority of gamers use cheats, they are far from oblivious to the implications of their actions. In fact, most players whom I have spoken to have devised intricate

honor codes for using cheats. While most of the players I interviewed admitted they used cheats, hardly any used them indis-
criminately. Instead, they opted to set conditions regulating their
use. Furthermore, cheating was used, for the most part, only in
order to engage with, rather than subvert, the game: most players
use cheats either to overcome a particular challenge that prevents
them from progressing in the game or to explore all the hidden
avenues a game has to offer.

Seen in this light, cheating has more than a few things in common with the Greek deus ex machina. Consider the following,
from Friedrich Nietzsche's *The Birth of Tragedy*:

> In their opening scenes Aeschylus and Sophocles
> employed the subtlest devices to give the spectator, as
> if by chance, all the threads that he would need for a
> complete understanding; a feature which preserves the
> noble artistry that masks the *necessary* formal element,
> making it look accidental. . . . Euripides . . . placed the
> prologue before the exposition and put it in the mouth
> of someone who could be trusted: a deity often had to
> guarantee the course of the tragedy to the audience, and
> remove any doubt as to the reality of the myth—just as
> Descartes could only prove the reality of the empiri-
> cal world by appealing to the veracity of God and His
> inability to lie. Euripides used this same divine veracity
> at the end of his drama, to guarantee the future of the
> protagonist to the audience. This was the purpose of
> the notorious *deus ex machina*.[32]

Euripides, in other words, left nothing to chance; for the audience to follow the plot in all its intricacy, a god had to spring out
of the machine. Unlike Aristotle, who insisted that the plot must
stem from the defining characteristics of the hero, Euripides was

not content with anything save for radical clarity; he devised a carefully constructed plot, first presented to and then summarized for the audience by the playwright's surrogate, the figure of absolute veracity, the god in the machine. While Aristotle, then, can be crowned the patron saint of games of emergence, Euripides's ghost hovers above video games, games of progression.

But the designer takes Euripides's dramaturgic sensibilities a step further, applying the deus ex machina not only for dramatic emphasis but rather as a mechanism of control. When stuck at some point in the game's progression, the novice player resorts to a cheat embedded by the designer to overcome the setback and continue to play. The cheat apparently emerges out of the belly of the machine. But, unlike the celestial gods at Euripides's disposal, revealing themselves in order to take charge, the designer's *dei ex machina* cloak themselves in order to reinstate order. The player is left to feel free and in control, a little guilty, and thoroughly engaged.

Here video games come closest to demonstrating their innate theological sensibilities: like religion, they offer a universe closely governed by rules yet one that recognizes the rules as merely the point of departure for an experience that is idiosyncratic and personally meaningful. This point is often lost on religion's loudest critics, for whom any organized expression of faith is an exercise in futility. Lenny Bruce captured this spirit well when he declared that more and more people were abandoning the church and going back to God, a juxtaposition that assumed a benign and benevolently anarchic creator on one end and a host of grim, oppressive nitpickers on the other. The Bruce doctrine, still very much in vogue today, points out that all religions face an inherent and unavoidable structural problem: to be holy, religion tells its followers, one must obey a series of rules, but when the rules descend from heaven and crash on earthly shores they immediately lose much of their absolutist might, if only because no human being could ever observe all of them meticulously. With human history being a dynamic and often irrational process, old rules are discarded and new ones are set in stone. Sects splinter off from main lines, differentiating themselves by rejecting this practice or consecrating that. That is how religion works. Talking about one's faith, then, any modern-day adherent to any major religion is often asked to defend not religion's theological underpinnings but its structural ones. If God is omnipotent, goes this taunt in its crudest form, why does God care what you eat or what you wear or when you pray? And if you believe your way is divinely sanctioned, mustn't it also mean that you necessarily view all others who fail to follow the same dictums as heathens, blasphemers, or worse? The Bruce doctrine solves this problem by celebrating a generalized form of spirituality, which demands nothing except the tentative willingness to embrace some undefined and indefinable form of higher power, no rules required. But this doctrine is a watered-down version not only of faith but also of thought: it ignores both the elasticity of the religious framework and its absolute necessity.

Hannah Arendt understood this point well. The Jews, she argued, were eventually granted full civil rights in their respective countries of residence, but in return were asked to abandon the ancient mystical yearnings for the promised land that have sustained them as a people for millennia. Once they did that, once they scrubbed their faith of its particularities, once they strove to tailor their religion to the needs and sensibilities of secular republics, they emptied Judaism of its meaning. To say, for example, that one believes in *tikkun olam*—a fantastically popular term nowadays, meaning, literally, repairing the world—is, in itself, meaningless, as no other belief system would ever claim to advance any other cause. Without the specific belief in messianic redemption and the series of rules that corresponded to it, secular Judaism's commitment to its former ideals dissolved into air, not because its practitioners believed in them any less, but because they had lost the sense of specificity, duty, and urgency that drove them to understand these ideals not as merely ethereal, universal principles but as a series of concrete and awesome commands. Being Jewish, Arendt argued, was only possible because of the particularities, because of the rules; without them, one isn't merely a lesser or unobservant Jew but not a Jew at all.

Such a strident argument, of course, invites objections, and those mostly depend on how one perceives the rules. See them as binding and unbreakable, as religion's endgame, and Arendt's argument forces out all but the most stringent and unquestioning practitioners of the faith. But see them as a starting point, and Spinoza, Einstein, Proust, and others whose relationships to their Judaism have been tormented happily rejoin the fray.

To better understand this point, let us return to the little boy whose act of cheating led off this chapter. As I observed him, he appeared to me a small Faust; following my basest instincts, I assumed that the game's rules were sacrosanct, and that the cheat code put the child in violation of the spirit of the game—which, I assumed, consisted merely of following the rules—and put anyone wishing to subvert it on the perilous path to soullessness. But I was wrong. The child wasn't Faust. He was James T. Kirk.

In a memorable moment in one of the *Star Trek* movies, the famous fictional Starfleet captain is presented with a notoriously difficult training drill. It is a simulation of a situation in which a civilian ship finds itself stranded in Klingon territory. Try to rescue it, and the Klingons will attack in retaliation. Abandon it, and the ship, along with its passengers, will not be spared. The drill is designed to examine how cadets handle no-win situations, but Kirk, taking his place on the simulated ship's bridge, is the first to succeed in rescuing the ship without provoking the Klingons. When asked by his amazed colleagues how he pulled off such a feat, he replies that he does not believe in no-win situations and had therefore reprogrammed the simulation's software in advance to allow for a third option.

You could look at Kirk's action as a cheat; he broke the academy's rules. But you could also argue that they reflect a higher order of systemic thinking and dedication. As a player, he does not, like Faust, see himself as lacking any agency unless awarded it by an external source. Instead, he reflects the wisdom of the Jewish sage Rabbi Akiva who argued that "everything is foreseen, and permission is granted." Rabbi Akiva and Captain Kirk both believe that there's a divine plan firmly in place, but they also know that each of us is allowed to mess with it, reject it, subvert it, and subject it to our own free will. Otherwise, everything—video games, religion, or being a Starfleet captain—would be robbed of its mysteries and charms and reduced to a series of strictures in the service of some divine force none of us will ever truly know.

With his cheat sheet at hand, then, the young boy innately understood several things. First, he realized that games, like religions, needed rules—that they were, in fact, rules—and that without rules, games would be solipsistic and confusing, leaving each of us to wonder what to do next. Second, and no less important, the boy grasped that by cheating he entered the game on his own terms, a flexible and sharp negotiator, no less reverent of the game but much more likely to carve within it a meaningful space for himself. It is a rejection of both fundamentalism and helplessness, not just a refusal to follow rules blindly but an understanding that following rules blindly was never the point. Like their most intelligent and agile practitioners, religions contain multitudes. And like the best video games, religions forge a host of elegant cheats and offer them as tools designed to further emotional engagement and facilitate individual exploration.

To understand this phenomenon in depth, we must call on that renowned video game enthusiast, Martin Heidegger.

The God Machine

ON BEING AND TIME IN VIDEO GAMES

Watching *Oedipus*, W. H. Auden tells us, the audience is stricken by a sense of tragedy that originates from witnessing the Greek follow the preordained path that leads him to doom. As Father is slain and Mother wed, the audience, Auden claims, whispers, "What a pity it had to happen this way."[1] But the same audience, watching Shakespeare's Scottish play, is likely to experience a sensation of an altogether different sort; witnessing Macbeth consider his options and then, of his own free will, favor a bloody, murderous path, the audience, writes Auden, sighs, "What a pity it was this way when it might have been otherwise."[2] This, the poet instructs us, is the fundamental difference between the Greek and the Christian tragic hero: the former is tragic because the hero has no choice, the latter precisely because the hero does.

Having carefully examined both the video game player and the video game designer, let us for a moment attempt to carry Auden's distinction further and ask what, if anything, a video game hero might look like. Where would such a character fall on Auden's scale? At first, such a proposition appears out of place. Video games, after all, are linear narratives in which the inevitable conclusion demands the character's—and therefore, the player's—ultimate triumph. The parlance of players speaks not of "finishing" the game but of "beating" it, meaning the successful completion of the game's main quest or task. Therefore, every video game narrative, even the most bleak, necessarily possesses that most untragic of characteristics, the happy ending. Seen in this light, no video game could ever be classified as a tragedy.

But video games have a strong tragic undercurrent that mustn't be ignored—one, indeed, that is essential to understanding the games not only as narratives but also the medium itself as whole. Before discussing video games as tragedy, then, let us first discuss tragedies as such.

For a hero to be considered tragic, Aristotle instructs us, four conditions must be met:[3] The first is nobility. The tragic hero, according to Aristotle, must be noble, regardless of class (suggesting even that such an accomplishment is possible for such base entities as women and slaves), meaning in pursuit of "goodness," manifested in compassion and a desire to seek the truth. With very few exceptions—the protagonists of the popular *Grand Theft Auto* series first and foremost among them—video game protagonists fit that description perfectly. By and large, video games, as narratives, have been largely uninfluenced by the modern penchant, in literature and film, for antiheroes; instead, the games' protagonists are noble at heart—that is, they embark on quests that pit them on the side of absolute good and in opposition to absolute evil—and, very frequently, are also noble by birth or by destiny. Nearly each one of the medium's iconic heroes fits that definition, from the humble plumber Mario who saves a princess and inherits a kingdom, to Master Chief, the armor-clad protagonist of the smash hit *Halo*, whose stature is so exalted that he was cryogenically frozen, to be revived only once the world is at the brink of doom. Or consider, for example, *The Legend of Zelda*'s Link, an orphan who grew up with kindly grandparents, and who, in maturity, discovers his true identity as a descendant of a long line of heroes who must now rise to the occasion and save the besieged Princess Zelda. To that end, at least two installments in the series—*The Minish Cap* and *The Wind Waker*—begin with an introductory sequence that features a mythic hero whose physical appearance is identical to that of Link's, with the implication being that Link is no ordinary mortal who had greatness thrust upon him by circumstance, but rather an incarnation of a transcendental and immortal benevolent spirit. This assertion is stated straightforwardly in the *Ocarina of Time*, the most popular installment in the series to date, in which Link is dubbed the latest in the line of Heroes of Time, the bravest of all mythical warriors in the game's universe. Video game heroes, then, are often noble.

But all tragic heroes must have tragic flaws that bring about their downfall, or hamartia. This characteristic is closely linked, if not identical, to hubris and is often found in video game protagonists. Nearly without exception, this moment lies outside of the player's control and is conveyed to the player in short, noninteractive sequences—brief animated films—that interrupt the flow of the game. Looking at *Zelda* once again, we witness Link, usually at the height of his combative prowess, committing grave errors time and again, the result of pride and arrogance. In *The Wind Waker*, for example, Link twice attempts to defeat Ganondorf, the king of evil and the series's ultimate antagonist, even after being told by friendly advisors that he lacks the means to defeat the malevolent enemy. In *Ocarina of Time* this narrative line goes even further when Link—again, as a result of hubris—inadvertently helps Ganondorf find the Triforce, a golden triangle that is the source of all courage, wisdom, and power in the game's world. Mario, perhaps the most recognizable video game protagonist, is similar in this respect, often brashly and proudly dismissing Bowser, his evil nemesis, only to witness, a short while later, a reinvigorated Bowser bouncing back, fortified and menacing as ever. Max Payne, the protagonist of the popular video game and motion picture series, allows himself, in the second game in the series (titled, appropriately, *The Fall of Max Payne*) to ignore all that he learned in the first installment and, self-assured and headstrong, plunge into yet another perilous adventure, one that sends him on a series of setbacks and diverts him from completing the game's main quest.

When good heroes do bad, they bring about peripeteia, or reversal of fortune. Again, Link provides an excellent example: when he tries to attack Ganondorf before he is ready for battle, he fails and nearly pays with his life. The failure shifts the focus of the game; from appearing to be on the verge of completing his quest— at each point, the ill-conceived battle with Ganondorf is framed as potentially the game's last such one—Link, and therefore the player, is now forced to undertake a new set of time-consuming and arduous tasks before facing Ganondorf again. Similarly, when he loses the Triforce to Ganondorf, he must set out on a quest to retrieve the lost object and once again face his nemesis. Even Tommy Vercetti, the protagonist of *Grand Theft Auto: Vice City*, one of the most popular games in the extremely successful series, is propelled to complete the game's various missions by an inevitable (that is to say, nonplayable, noninteractive) series of bad decisions. In every turn, the designers feature Vercetti taking the less-accommodating path, until he is eventually forced to eliminate all of his former friends and colleagues in order to escape elimination himself.

What follows is anagnorisis, or the hero's knowledge or awareness that his reversal of fortune is the result of his own doing. Link, for example, follows his misdeeds with a short speech, lamenting his bad judgment and its unfortunate consequences. Vercetti does the same.

These examples, to be sure, do not occur throughout the course of game play—namely, as events brought about by the player's own actions—but, again, are conveyed to the player through noninteractive opening sequences, interstitials, and other measures that are designed strictly to enhance and further plot, not playability. Theoretically, in all of the aforementioned cases, the designers could have advanced the plot linearly and without complications, yet the designers chose to introduce into the game an element of fault. The hardships the hero encounters, the games suggest, are not inflicted for no apparent reason, but are rather brought forth by the hero's own hand, at least to some extent. This approach, again, corresponds perfectly to Aristotle's edicts, claiming that inflicting suffering on a wholly virtuous hero, or good fortune on a wholly evil one, arouses in the audience not empathy but repulsion. Video game protagonists are no exception to this rule, and instances of hamartia are woven into narrative after narrative.

This, however, presents us with an enigma. Until now, we have come to see video games as a medium defined by linearity, inevitability, and flow. We have discussed intention as the mechanism designed to create an illusion of free will while gently guiding the player down a singular—and unavoidable—path. We have also identified playability, rather than storytelling or plotting, as the chief concern of video games, and we have seen how the former is often subjugated in service of the latter. Why, then, hamartia? Why, in other words, in game after game, introduce a fundamentally flawed hero?

At first glance, the logic behind such decisions appears sound. Video game protagonists must be flawed for the same reason literary or cinematic heroes must be flawed—meaning for the very reasons dictated by Aristotle: namely, to secure the player's empathy rather than have the player quit in disgust at the sight of a hapless and perfect hero afflicted with unjust and unreasonable pain. But unlike other narratives, video games possess plots designed to play, a notion rendered more difficult by the introduction of tragic elements.[4] Hamartia, after all, as Nancy Sherman keenly observes, is nothing if not "missing the target";[5] Oedipus, for example, misses his target by killing a man he takes for an insolent stranger and whom he later discovers was his father. The logic of hamartia, therefore, is the logic of the incidental, or even the accidental; Aristotle himself clearly refers to accidents as a particular subcategory of hamartia. Why, then, would video games choose this precarious element as a fixture when plotlines exist mainly to serve playability? Why would a medium in which nothing is accidental choose the accident as one of the main tools with which to progress the narrative and around which to construct novel scenarios with which the player could then interact?

While several explanations may provide partial answers—all, I believe, revolving around the dictates of storytelling—one in particular appears plausible, addressing, as it does, video games not as a subcategory of narratives that happen, almost as an afterthought, to be played out, but rather as playthings that happen to tell stories. This theory, too, has to do with intention. Since, as demonstrated earlier in this work, players form an emotional attachment to the characters they are playing—an attachment created largely through the physical realm, the player's movements being that of the character and vice versa—hamartia serves to create in the player a sensation of culpability. Even though the tragic incident (or accident)—confronting a nemesis while ill-prepared, say, ignoring warnings, or any of the aforementioned misdeeds—always occurs in the course of a noninteractive sequence, the player—prone to seeing the game's character as an extension of himself—is charged with resolving the complications that arise from one's own hamartia. In other words, just as I came to describe in the first-person singular events that occurred to Link within the context of the game I was playing, once the noninteractive sequence is over, the player has no choice but to suffer the consequences of the errors in which the player had no hand. The player, for example, might have refrained from fighting Ganondorf, but once the designer decreed that Link would prematurely fight his nemesis, the player must resume control and deal with the consequences. It is now a personal fight.

Hamartia thus becomes an interesting mechanism of intention.

By revolving the plot around seminal flaws that lie beyond the player's control, but which the player must nevertheless address and rectify, the designer creates a peculiar hybrid of both of Auden's tragic heroes. Like Oedipus, the player, as Link, has no control over Link's fate; he is left to witness predestined events unfurling all around him, events whose outcome the player is unable to influence or alter. But once the noninteractive sequence is over and the player is again happily pressing buttons, intention takes its toll, and the player feels a sensation of control. Now, the player is no more Oedipus but Macbeth; despite having had no hand in the error, the player never stops to question the unfolding of the plot. Rather, the player accepts the hamartia as inevitable and the responsibility for it. The player, in other words, accepts hamartia as something of one's own doing, a wrong choice that was made when, perhaps, a right one was always possible, a fault the consequences of which one must now suffer. Just as cheating is always inherent in the game but nonetheless is often defined by the players as transgressive—thereby transforming a value-neutral act into one with moral implications—so does the plot, by adopting tragic elements, drive the player to feel personally responsible for rectifying that which demands rectification. In so doing, the designer resembles Pyotr Stepanovich Verkhovensky, the nefarious villain of Dostoevsky's *Demons*, who forced his colleagues to commit a terrible crime in order to guarantee their future cooperation. Just as Verkhovensky cemented his colleagues' fealty by making them culpable, so does the designer construct plots utilizing tragic elements. By so doing, the designer secures the player's future commitment, as the plot's trajectory set forth by the designer is now perceived by the player to have been the direct result of free will.

Yet the player never truly becomes either Oedipus or Macbeth; rather, the player is left to follow the designer's detailed formulation, playing the game to its (inevitably happy) end. There are, in other words, no consequences to the hamartia; the peripeteia is met with a countering force, once again reversing the fortunes of the game's protagonist, this time away from tragedy and toward resolution. What began as a tragedy ends as an epic poem, the hero having successfully completed the quest.

And yet, this moment of counterperipeteia, too—this moment in which the tragic flaw is suddenly corrected—also occurs outside the realm of the player's control. Having accepted responsibility for the hero's downfall and pursued the game in order to reverse the bitter fate, the player will once again encounter a noninteractive sequence in which all is corrected. Link, for example, having twice attempted to defeat Ganondorf while ill-prepared—and having been thrust into battle in a noninteractive sequence and left, in both cases, with no choice but to react to the detrimental consequences—will suddenly be presented with another noninteractive sequence in which he is informed that he now possesses the necessary powers to defeat the villain. Mario, too, is, in three different installments, informed by various characters in the game that Bowser, having been reinvigorated by Mario's own miscalculations, is now ripe for the taking. And Max Payne finishes the first installment in the series atop a building, where a sudden thunderstorm, erupting as he kicks open the door to a rooftop in pursuit of his nemesis, enables him to shoot down his nemesis's helicopter and thereby end the game. As the main quest is completed, every game provides a brief noninteractive sequence—a short animated movie clip during which the player cannot interact with the game but only watch—ensuring us that the protagonist's future is one of peace and prosperity.

But noninteractive sequences are not the only places where the designer shapes the game's moral center of gravity. Another useful element is repetition. Like Sisyphus, the ancient Greek rock carrier, the player is also primarily engaged, throughout most of the game play experience, in going through the same motions again and again and again. The overwhelming majority of video games, it bears repeating, are designed as linear narratives consisting of a series of challenges, with the player successfully completing each one in order to advance to the next. Nearly always, a challenge will not be resolved right away; an enjoyable game, after all, must have a component of difficulty, and intention works best when it requires the player to posit a few theories pertaining to the solution of a specific problem before solving it. And while attempting different approaches, the player is essentially repeating the same play section again and again, with very little—if any—concrete variation. As discussed in the first two chapters of this work, such repetition is instrumental to the nature of video game design; in everything from the limited number of potential enemies and movement sequences to the need to retry and overcome portions of the game at which the player had been unsuccessful, the logic of video game play is that of repetition.

The first association evoked here might very well be one of trance; repetition, after all, is a crucial component in trance or trancelike situations, and video games provide not only repetitive situations and repetitive formulations but also a physical sense of repetition, with the player continuously repeating a limited number of motions and actions, primarily with one's thumbs and fingers. But trance is not an apt description of the effects of repetition on the player. Unlike the entranced, the player never truly loses awareness of one's conscious self; while that self might merge, to an extent, with the character on screen, it is never completely lost. In other words, I may write in my journal that "I" did this or the other when in fact it was merely my actions guiding Link, my on-screen avatar, but at no point do I wholly abandon the distinction between myself and him. Furthermore, trancelike repetition—a major characteristic, for example, in surrealist art[6]—has the capacity for—and, often, the effect of—estrangement, the repetition rubbing the original object raw until it is stripped of its traditional, acquired meaning and ready to be assigned a new one. For video game designers, such estrangement, if it occurred, would necessarily be harmful, interrupting the flow of play that could only occur in a game environment that the player perceives as familiar and therefore navigable.

Rather than trance, then, repetition in video games revolves, I believe, around a bipartite paradox pertaining to movement and knowledge and inherited, unsurprisingly, from the Greeks. The first part of the paradox pertains to movement and is a design-centric paraphrase of Zeno's paradox: the video game player, too, might feel as if movement—that is to say, progress—in video games is an impossibility, at least theoretically, as successfully completing the game's final task requires having completed the task before it, and as successfully completing the penultimate task requires having overcome the task before that, and so on. The player, therefore, is engaging a constantly fragmented reality; to the extent that video games do tell stories in the traditional sense of the word, this is a serious barrier, as the flow of the narrative is constantly interrupted by the challenges at hand. Even as muscle memory kicks in and one plays more fluidly, achieving a coherent idea of just where one is located in the game's long and convoluted plot is very difficult.

Unlike films and television shows, which, for the most part, adhere to certain conventions, at least as long as length is concerned, there is no set length for video games. Designers usually release their estimates pertaining to the play time the game might require for a moderately skilled player to complete the main quest; these estimations, however, might range from ten or fifteen hours in the case of relatively uncomplicated games to one hundred hours or more for more advanced, layered fare. The time estimate, however, is entirely subjective; the game, by its nature, consists of disparate challenges that different players might process differently (hence, again, the logic of the cheats as a regulating mechanism). The player, therefore, has no ability to estimate the true nature of one's own progression; unlike movies or television shows, no narrative-related conventions come to a player's aid. Whereas a movie, for example, might offer a few key plotlines that need to be resolved prior to the movie's ending, thereby giving the viewer a general, if vague, idea of the plot's progression, video games vary widely in length and scope. *The Ocarina of Time*, for example, an earlier installment of *The Legend of Zelda* series, comprises ten distinct levels, each one divided into three or four minilevels, while *The Twilight Princess*, a later installment, has only six distinct levels. The player, then, is thrust forward from one challenge to the next without any concept of when the quest might end. In so doing, the player never occupies a temporal magnitude but rather a disparate collection of nows.

This, of course, is more than an allusion to Zeno's other famous paradox, that of the archer and his arrow. Aristotle defines it thusly: "If everything when it occupies an equal space is at rest, and if that which is in locomotion is always occupying such a space at any moment, the flying arrow is therefore motionless."[7] For Aristotle, time comprises indivisible nows, and therefore, despite the arrow's being at rest at any given instance, it nevertheless moves. The video game player, however, does not traverse a horizon of indivisible nows but rather struggles to complete each now, each moment, each unit, as it arises. The player is therefore, metaphorically speaking, in perpetual movement and yet perpetually stuck.

Conversely, the player succumbs to a similar paradox in all matters pertaining to the acquisition of knowledge in the game's world. Hypothesizing on how the individual acquires knowledge, Plato, on several occasions, suggests that the soul, having originated from heaven, has witnessed there all things in their divine form and is therefore capable of recognizing them in their particular forms down on earth, a recognition triggered by the senses. This, of course, raises a paradox: if anything that could be learned is already known, then learning itself appears futile, a paradox that Plato resolves by repositioning learning as recollection. As discussed at length during the phenomenological section of this work, learning in video games is primarily recollection. New challenges and new enemies depend not on the acquisition of a new skill set—that would require allowing for constant learning curves, which would drive play time up considerably and turn games into cumbersome ordeals—but rather on the recollection of an ur-skill acquired early in the game or, in some cases, acquired outside the context of the game and understood as a general truth pertaining to video games—the knowledge, for example, that every jump will always reach the same height and last the same time. The challenges, in other words, are innovative and new, but the solutions are always the same. Never is the player required to do anything but recollect and repeat a fundamental—and basic—set of skills.

What, then, is the meaning of this repetition? A simple formulation would be to claim that the player truly does live in the moment. Consider, for example, the protagonist of Søren Kierkegaard's *Repetition*; despite his deep love for a young woman, he decides not to marry her, opting instead for a life dominated by obsessive—and repetitive—pondering of his beloved:

> Recollection's love, an author . . . has said, is the only happy love. He is perfectly right in that, of course, provided one recollects that initially it makes a person unhappy. Repetition's love is in truth the only happy love. Like recollection's love, it does not have the restlessness of hope, the uneasy adventurousness of discovery, but neither does it have the sadness of recollection—it has the blissful security of the moment.[8]

The statement, of course, presents a logical fallacy, one of many that Kierkegaard packs into his strange and difficult little book.

To experience something as repetition, one must first appeal to recollection; in other words, without remembering the initial occurrence, one has no way of perceiving its recurrence as such. Repetition, therefore, secures one's place in a perpetual moment— a moment, that is, that happens again and again—and yet it is an impossibility without a realization of the past that preceded it. Repetition and recollection, Kierkegaard informs us, are similar movements but in different directions, repetition moving forward and recollection back.[9]

Similarly, the video game player, like Zeno's arrow, is trapped in a series of moments, the connection between which the player is unable to perceive, yet the very skills that the player requires in order to successfully navigate the world of the game depend heavily on recollection. Video game time, therefore, emerges as an odd construct, a series of disparate moments that nonetheless require a past to bind them, a movement forward and backward occurring simultaneously. This, Kierkegaard suggests in his book, is the nature of aesthetics; the enamored subject of his book comes to experience his beloved aesthetically—incessantly writing poetry to her, experiencing her, therefore, not as a concrete other but rather as sublimated form—rather than ethically, which would have been the case had they married, leading him to assume the responsibility toward her that one assumes toward another subject. The nature of aesthetic experience is here understood, therefore, as magical precisely because it happens in the now but depends on the past for meaning; is already known and yet must be relearned again, sensually; and is a perfect wedding between the paradoxes of Zeno and Plato.

All media, to an extent, succumb to this seemingly paradoxical logic, and every media consumer is subjected to it. The television viewer, for example, is exposed to repetition and recollection simultaneously, with content appearing on screen that is at the same time new, the same, and dependent on prior knowledge to fully grasp; even one perusing hard news senses this to some degree, with news consisting of elements of both the innovative and the familiar.[10] Media consumers, then, digest information by assuaging the shock of the new with the balm of the familiar. But the video game player is unique among media consumers, as interaction with the medium, as we shall soon see, is not one of an analyzing subject but rather a participant in the narrative's creation. As such, the player, unlike the television viewer, lacks the ability to reconcile the aforementioned paradox by distancing from it, using Cartesian dualism as a wall between reality and its perception and reorganization in the subject's mind, but is rather in the thick of things, and therefore inhabiting time differently than others.

Video games' perception of time, to be sure, isn't new. It was first posited by Plato, who, true to his theory of forms, saw time as a duality: *chronos*, or time as we perceived it in the world of the senses, and *aion*, an idealized form of time, or, as the theologian Jeremy Begbie put it, the "mode of being of the Ideas in which past, present, and future coincide in one."[11] *Aion*, then, isn't abstract; it possesses, Begbie notes, "the structure, though not the movement, of time."[12] Taking his cues from Plato, Augustine's concept of time was similarly bifurcated: we are only capable of experiencing the present, he argued, but our minds contain also the past and the future. "Some such different times do exist in the mind," he wrote, "in nowhere else that I can see. The presence of past things is memory, the presence of present things is direct apprehension, the presence of future things is expectation."[13] Therefore, as the theologian Brian Leftow argued, Augustine was moved by Neo-platonist metaphysics to believe that "nobody has true being, pure being, real being except one who does not change,"[14] and the only one who never changes, naturally, is the creator: "And I viewed the other things below you," Augustine wrote, "and I saw that neither can they be said absolutely to be or absolutely not to be. They are because they come from you. But they are not, because they are not what you are. That which truly is is that which unchangeably abides."[15]

Video game players have a similar understanding of time. Living in repetition, they are always changing yet always the same. They are, to paraphrase Augustine, because the designer is—a radically different approach than that argued by the interpreting individualists. To understand this approach better, I now embark on a brief discussion of the subjectivity of the video game player, relying heavily on Martin Heidegger's *Sein und Zeit*.

While my purpose here is not to delve deeply into abstract philosophical issues but rather to appropriate their theoretical frameworks and, in some cases, language, to address the distinct realities of video games, I am nonetheless compelled to offer a brief introduction to Heideggerian thought, focusing, of course, solely on those aspects that later emerge as instructive. I keep the discussion brief, however, refraining from any complications unrelated to the subject at hand.

Heidegger's main movement in *Sein und Zeit* is in opposition to Descartes. The latter, with his "*Cogito ergo sum*," not only asserts a duality of mind and body but also positions—as did Kant and Hume—the individual as a spectator of, rather than an actor in, the world. While, without doubt, occupying a physical world and interacting with physical things—Descartes himself holds his ball of wax—the individual is nonetheless essentially excluded from any concrete action occurring in the world, not inhabiting it in any concrete sense but rather watching it and later reconstructing it as an image in one's own head. In so doing, humans possess the transcendental freedom usually associated with God.[16] Descartes, Heidegger claims, portrays Man's inhabiting the World as water does a glass, a faulty framework for two reasons. While the glass could be emptied of the water without fundamentally affecting the nature of either, the same could not be said of Man and the World; and Man, unlike the glass and the water both, is aware of the encounter with the world and does not merely coexist with it as one object beside another—or, for that matter, as subject to object. If that were the case, as Stephen Mulhall notes in his guide to *Sein und Zeit*, a "closet of consciousness" would be erected, preventing the subject from ever emerging "from its inner sanctum into the external, public realm whose entities with their properties are the supposed object of its 'knowledge.'"[17] Circumventing this problem, Heidegger supposes a state of knowing as being-in-the-world; "If I 'merely' know about some way in which the Being of entities is interconnected . . . I am no less alongside the entities outside in the world than when I originally grasp them."[18]

This point becomes clearer once we consider Heidegger's famous distinction between presence-at-hand and readiness-to-hand. Consider, for example, the following passage:

> Hammering does not simply have knowledge about the hammer's character as equipment, but it has appropriated this equipment in a way that could not possibly be more suitable. . . . The less we just stare at the hammer-thing, and the more we seize hold of it and use it, the more primordial does our relationship to it become, and the more unveiledly is it encountered as that which it is—as equipment. The hammering itself uncovers the specific "manipulability" of the hammer. The kind of Being which equipment possesses—in which it manifests itself in its own right—we call *readiness-to-hand*.[19]

In other words, it is not enough for one to observe a hammer—or, for that matter, someone else hammering—to grasp the hammer-ness of the hammer-thing; for that, one must pick up a hammer and drive a nail through a wall. Only then is the hammerness of the hammer-thing fully experienced as such.

Heidegger takes this idea even further: not only does he make the distinction between presence-at-hand (the state of knowing things and their uses) and readiness-to-hand, but he maintains that every object ultimately exists "in-order-to," meaning with a specific serviceability in mind, and that this serviceability always has a similar purpose, namely the being of *Dasein* (or there-being, the name by which Heidegger calls any human individual, wishing to stress not its autonomous subjectivity but its state of being-in-the-world):

> With the "towards-which" of serviceability there can again be an involvement: with this thing, for instance, which is ready-to-hand and which we accordingly call a "hammer," there is an involvement in hammering; with hammering there is an involvement in making something fast; with making something fast, there is an involvement in protection against bad weather; and this protection "is" for the sake of providing shelter for Dasein—that is to say, for the sake of a possibility of Dasein's Being.[20]

This observation is not without its radical implications. For Heidegger, to name the issue most prevalent to our discussion, space exists not as it does for Descartes, namely as a fixed grid with exact coordinates, but rather as a derivative of readiness-to-handness. As Mulhall explains it:

> Dasein most fundamentally understands its spatial relations with objects as a matter of near and far, close and distant; and these in turn are understood in relation to its practical purposes. The spectacles on my nose

> are further away from me than the picture on the wall
> that I use them to examine, and the friend I see across
> the road is nearer to me than the pavement under my
> feet; my friend would not have been any closer to me
> if she had appeared at my side, and moving right up to
> the picture would in fact distance it from me. Closeness
> and distance in this sense are a matter of handiness and
> unhandiness; the spatial disposition of the manifold of
> objects populating my environment is determined by
> their serviceability for my current activities.[21]

This assertion, too, fortifies the main characteristic of *Dasein*. Unlike, say, inanimate objects, or even animals—which, according to Heidegger, merely exist without giving any thought to the fact that they do—*Dasein* is the only living being for whom its being is an issue, and, as such, its being is a fundamental issue for *Dasein*, one that dictates all others, including those previously seen as natural and neutral, such as spatiality.

Two more observations about *Dasein* must be raised before we can apply Heidegger's theory to better understand the ontological nature of video game play. First of all, building on his observations concerning the inherent serviceability of objects, Heidegger recognizes that the same could be also said about *Dasein*. Just as we understand the objects surrounding us primarily in terms of their use-value—namely, the understanding of a hammer not for some abstract "hammerness" but rather for its serviceability in driving nails into surfaces—we must also understand ourselves first and foremost as practitioners. Now, as Mulhall observes, no practice can exist unless it is practiced by many; there could never be a practice practiced by a solitary individual, just as, to paraphrase Wittgenstein, one could never follow a rule privately. A rule is a rule precisely because it applies to all. Heidegger, then, makes a bold statement about the true nature of *Dasein*:

The Self of everyday Dasein is the they-self, which we distinguish from the authentic Self—that is, from the Self which has been taken hold of in its own way. As they-self, the particular Dasein has been dispersed into the "they," and must first find itself.[22]

But every being capable of finding itself, as Mulhall notes, must also be capable of losing itself, and such losing is definitive of *Dasein*'s day-to-day existence. Describing mundane actions such as utilizing public transportation and reading the newspaper, Heidegger claims that, in such situations,

> every other is like the next. This Being-with-one-another dissolves one's own Dasein completely into the kind of Being of "the Others," in such a way, indeed, that the Others, as distinguishable and explicit, vanish more and more.[23]

Dasein, then, is not merely a member of a collective of Others, a crowd consisting of distinct *Dasein*s with distinct tastes, ideas, and sensibilities. Rather, due to the interchangeability of subjectivity, *Dasein* persists in a they-self existence, the "they" being no less ephemeral than *Dasein*. This leads Heidegger to a radical assertion: *Dasein*'s being is inherently inauthentic.

There is, however, one moment at which *Dasein* might gain authenticity: the moment of death. As the only form of being imminently aware of its own being, *Dasein*, Heidegger claims, lives life as a movement *toward* death; death, therefore, is not what matters, but *dying*, or the manner in which the being lives aiming toward death. But dying, unlike every other interchangeable experience, cannot be experienced; mourning, therefore, is impossible in Heidegger's eyes, as we cannot experience death ourselves and therefore cannot comprehend it in others. Dying, therefore, is the moment in which *Dasein* can claim authenticity; "every Dasein," Heidegger informs us, "must actually take dying upon itself."[24] Death, in other words, is the only action that I cannot undertake for you or you for me; we must experience it alone, or, better yet, experience it never, for death cannot be stored in *Dasein*'s quiver of experiential arrows. It is rather, quite simply, the end of *Dasein*. *Dasein* only becomes him- or herself when ceasing to be.

The dying of *Dasein*, Heidegger therefore suggests, can be likened to a ripening of a fruit, running its course, always not-ripe until it's ripe. *Dasein*, Heidegger formulates, "is always already its not yet, as long as it is."[25] But unlike fruit, which in ripening reaches the fullest extent of its being, *Dasein*, at the moment of ceasing to be not-yet, is no more. And, unlike fruit once again, nothing guarantees *Dasein* that he or she will ever be able to fulfill one's full potential. *Dasein* could perish without having acted on even a sliver of one's potential; this is why Heidegger suggests that as soon as he or she is born, *Dasein* is old enough to die.

We now possess a sufficient theoretical framework into which to try and order the video game player. Speaking in 1938, a decade after *Sein und Zeit*, before a crowd of laypersons, Heidegger made the following comment: "Once the world has become an image," he said, "the human position grasps itself as Weltanschauung,"[26] the latter term often translated as "worldview." Yet it is not worldview that Heidegger was concerned with, but another term, similar in name yet divergent in nature—the *Weltbild*, or the world-picture. The story of modernity, Heidegger insisted, was not that of interchangeable worldviews struggling for prominence but rather of mankind's attempt to "conquer the world as image."[27] Thusly, Heidegger posits a rigid commitment, for, as Samuel Weber notes, "To determine the world as having the structure of a picture or image is thus to embark upon a project of conquest in which the heterogeneity of being is accepted only insofar as it can be objectified and represented."[28] In this context Heidegger made the major conceptual move of the lecture, urging his listeners to embark on a quest for *Nennkraft*, or the originary naming power. For Heidegger, this power, or force, revolves around oscillation; its two major movements are the setting of things in front of oneself and the bringing of things out in front of oneself, two nearly identical moves—the former being more external in nature and the latter internal, both requiring a strong, willing subject at the center. Both movements yield similar results. This, according to Heidegger, is the fundamental essence of technology: *Bestellbarkeit*, or the ability of being placed and displaced at will, on order, on demand. The world, therefore, is now a picture "whose ultimate function is to establish and confirm the centrality of man as the being capable of depiction."[29] The subject, in other words, becomes the reference point of things as such.

This formulation, written with cinema in mind, should not be foreign to any avid television watcher. Television watching, after all, is an experience that demands and places at its heart a subject who, with a click of a button, commands the images on screen back and forth. The distance between screen and sofa is, indeed, the critical distance between the Cartesian empirical universe and its re-creation in the subject's mind. As was once and again demonstrated by scores of researchers in both cultural and communications studies, such a distance creates ample space for interpretation and reinterpretations. Consider the following example, the renowned study by Elihu Katz and Tamar Liebes concerning divergent meanings assigned to a commonly viewed episode of the television series *Dallas*. Sitting in a living room along with several couples, a researcher observed the conversation that unfolded before, during, and after the broadcast, noting that each participant, despite the communal experience of viewing, nonetheless interpreted the meaning of the episode according to his or her own preexisting set of cultural, religious, and socioeconomic biases. As Katz and Liebes note:

This group is of particular interest because it illustrates
vividly how community members negotiate meanings
by confronting the text with their own tradition and
their own experience. The conversation suggests that
the program serves viewers as a forum for discussion of
personal, interpersonal and social issues such as justice;
whether or not fathers have equal rights in their children; child-rearing problems; gender-role differences;
attitudes towards adultery and divorce; the problem of
cramped quarters; religious demands; and the harsh
reality of prolonged war in Lebanon. Consider also the
references to other texts—especially religious ones.[30]

The viewers in this case are subjects, capable of depiction at will,
constructing their own world-picture.

The video game player could not be more different. He is not
a Cartesian subject but a Heideggerian *Dasein*; his only being is
being-in-the-world. Unlike television, which continues to broadcast even as one shuts off the machine, the video game begins
when the player turns on the machine and ends when the player
turns it off; the player comes into being as a player, therefore, only
when the world of the game comes into being as a game. The video
game player, again, has nothing to do with Nietzsche's interpretations; the player follows rules, which keep the player in a perpetual
state not too dissimilar from religious observance. Such a state,
Heidegger believed, was always true of *Dasein*. "No one is without religion," he told a documentary film crew interviewing him.
"And every person in a certain way transcends themselves, that
is, they are displaced."[31] Heidegger had little explicit to say about
religion, and much of what he did say had to do with how not to
try and understand it. In a lecture course he gave in 1921 and 1922
on the subject, he argued that a philosophy or religion was bound
to fail if it argued that religion "should be philosophically under-

stood, conceptualized," and that religion had to be "projected into intelligible context."[32] The only thing religion demanded of us, he argued, is *Nachfolge*, or following the words of the founder, Christ. In this, he echoes Luther, who argued that *Nachfolge* "must proceed not according to your understanding, but beyond your understanding."[33]

According to Heidegger's understanding, however, Christianity, or any other religion, still offers room for interpretation. As Robert Metcalf points out in his essay on Heidegger's concept of *Nachfolge*, Christianity offers a "hermeneutic openness"[34] that stems in part from its founder having himself radically departed from his own inherited religious traditions. What, then, might following the founder mean?

The thought might have displeased Heidegger, but his view of religion, as it appears in the few addresses on the subject he left behind, isn't necessarily far from Augustine's. In the fifth century, the church father found himself under attack from an unexpected source, a British monk named Pelagius. Around the year 405, Pelagius caught wind of Augustine's famous *Confessions*; one quote in particular seized his attention. "Give me what you command," Augustine wrote, "and command what you will." To Pelagius, such talk emptied people of all meaning, turning them into mere automatons. In response, he fashioned a doctrine of his own.

"Whenever I have to speak on the subject of moral instruction and conduct of a holy life, it is my practice first to demonstrate the power and quality of human nature and to show what it is capable of achieving, and then to go on to encourage the mind of my listener to consider the idea of different kinds of virtues, in case it may be of little or no profit to him to be summoned to pursue ends which he has perhaps assumed hitherto to be beyond his reach," he stated in one of his letters. "For we can never end upon the path of virtue unless we have hope as our guide and compassion. . . . Any good of which human nature is capable has to be revealed, since what is shown to be practicable must be put into practice."[35] In other words, Pelagius believed that God gave human beings the will to live a sinless, unblemished life. This, of course, meant doing away with the notion of original sin, as well as relegating Christ to a fairly marginal role.

Reading Pelagius's work, Augustine was livid. He responded with a series of letters of his own. One quote, written in 412, captures Augustine's argument well: "What merits of his own has the saved to boast of when, if he were dealt with according to his merits, he would be nothing if not damned? Have the just then no merits at all? Of course they do, for they are the just. But they had no merits by which they were made just." In other words, the only thing saving Man from eternal damnation is God's grace, expressed most profoundly in Christ, whose sacrifice was a gift the Lord bestowed on God's undeserving and wretched children.

Augustine emerged the victor, going on, in the famous words of his contemporary, Jerome, to "establish anew the ancient faith." Poor Pelagius, on the other hand, was banished from Rome and headed to Palestine, where he most likely died. It is easy for us moderns to question the wisdom of history's judgment. It would appear, after all, that Pelagius is offering a thoroughly enlightened doctrine: we are each infused with the divine spirit and therefore each free to be the masters of our own fate, leading ourselves either toward redemption or into damnation. But such an approach is far more rigid than it sounds; it places upon people an onus no individual could bear. No lesser mind than James Madison understood this principle well. "If men were angels," Madison wrote in *The Federalist Papers*,

> no government would be necessary. If angels were to govern men, neither external nor internal controls on government would be necessary. In framing a government which is to be administered by men over men,

the great difficulty lies in this: you must first enable the government to control the governed; and in the next place oblige it to control itself. A dependence on the people is, no doubt, the primary control on the government; but experience has taught mankind the necessity of auxiliary precautions.[36]

Augustine, on the other hand, offered a much more humane approach to the question: while life under the shadow of the original sin might appear unjust, divine grace emerges to kindle the torch that illuminates the path to redemption.

Video game players, as we've seen, live constantly with original sins. They are plagued by plot turns over which they had no control. They are trapped in a world they can never really shape. Their will is a strange and fragile thing. But whereas their brethren—television viewers and book readers and art admirers—are left merely with the infinite frustration that emanates from endless interpretation, longing for communion and seething at its impossibility, video game players are guided by grace. The designer, through the game, teaches us that the true joy is the joy of learning, of our own free will, to love the game and the designer above all, to abandon all other ways of being in the world, all other claims on subjectivity or agency, and instead embrace the true happiness that comes with understanding one's place in the world. I am speaking here, of course, metaphorically; not for one moment do I intend to equate a mortal video game designer with the supreme being. But the ontological condition of the game player, I believe, closely reflects this Augustinian condition, the condition that a wide array of thinkers—from Maimonides with his insistence on religious observance to Heidegger with his praise for the same—have upheld. Put crudely, the formulation would be, as Heidegger indeed implied, that the only way to overcome the malaise brought about by the technological age would be to revert to Christian thought (or, in a Maimonidean spin, Jewish thought). Video games, then, should be seen as an Augustinian simulator, a rule-based environment into which one enters, abandoning the pursuit of reason and receiving instead a chance to transcend the irresolvable anxieties of modern media.

Irresolution is precisely the point. As all art rattles toward resolution, video games, with their state of being in the moment, are the medium devoted to tension. As such, they are fertile soil for the teaching of an ethically nuanced worldview. "Well-handled maintenance of tensions is ethically desired," the philosopher Kathleen Marie Higgins argued, and is "essential to living a balanced, happy life."[37] She then praised music for helping us achieve a spiritual balance as it "presents tensions, not as obstructions, but as themselves vehicles to the achievement of resolution."[38] In other words, a life lived to the fullest is dedicated not to the endless pursuit of stasis, but rather to the embodiment of tension. If any human technology has the chance of teaching us this art, it is video games.

The time has come, then, to abandon all of our old prejudices and see video games in light of what they are. Far from shoving youths into spirals of violent behavior (a repeatedly and rather thoroughly refuted canard), video games provide that rarest of havens, an environment in which to learn, without fear of consequence, how to live differently—not retreating into modernity's guessing games and solipsistic pleasures but stepping, however hesitatingly, into an order governed by the same ideas and the same beliefs that have guided the species for millennia, experiencing, with our bodies and our minds, not anxiety but joy, not doubt but faith, not just the prickly self but the world entire.

Acknowledgments

First and foremost, this book is dedicated to the late Frank Moretti, a singular teacher and a kind friend who understood better than most that those enamored with the vagaries of technology had no better guides than the ancients, who often asked, and sometimes answered, the very same questions as us. I miss him, and am sad to think of this book as the last exchange in a great and joyous conversation Frank and I had had for years.

Intellectual pursuits like the one represented in this book require a great deal of freedom and a greater deal of support, and I was very fortunate to receive both in Columbia University's unparalleled doctoral program in communications. There, I enjoyed not only the support of my talented peers and the benefit of learning from their diverse interests, but also the shepherding of a few remarkable scholars and thinkers: John Pemberton, Michael Taussig, and James Schamus, whatever merits this book may have are a testament to your influence. Above all, Todd Gitlin, my mentor and my dear friend, shared with me his wisdom and his warmth, both of which continue to inspire and sustain me.

Having spent the last three years at New York University, I am grateful to my colleagues who took an interest in my work and set an example with stellar work of their own: Mary Brabeck; Beth Weitzman; Marita Sturken; Ted Magder; Lisa Gitelman; Terry Moran; Russ Neuman; Chris Hoadley; Jan Plass; Joost van Dreunen; Max Foxman; Aurora Wallace; Aaron Cohen; Melissa

Lucas; Dove Pedlosky; and Alexa Pearce. I am equally as indebted to my students, whose passion, intelligence, and spirit fuels my work.

In the long process of translating my ideas and research into a language spoken by more than a few of us zealous monks, I owe the deepest gratitude to Anne Edelstein, my incomparable agent and guardian angel, and to Adam Bellow, whose endless intellectual horizons drove me to strive and widen my own.

Finally, I am endlessly indebted to the love of my life, Lisa Sandell, and our amazing children, Lily and Hudson, without whom no game is worth playing.

Notes

An Invocation

1. William S. Burroughs, "Apocalypse," http://www.spress.de/author/bur roughs/texts/prose/apoc.htm.

Chapter 1: Thinking inside the Box

1. An earlier version of this argument has appeared in *The New Republic* (Liel Leibovitz, "MoMA Has Mistaken Video Games for Art," March 13, 2013). Available online at http://www.newrepublic.com/article/112646 /moma-applied-design-exhibit-mistakes-video-games-art.

2. See Ervin Goffman, *The Presentation of the Self in Everyday Life* (New York: Doubleday, 1959).

3. Rudy Bretz, *Media for Interactive Communication* (Beverly Hills, CA: Sage Publications, 1983); quoted in Jerome T. Durlak, "A Typology for Interactive Media," in Margaret L. McLaughlin (ed.), *Communication Yearbook 10* (Newbury Park, CA: Sage Publications, 1987), 744.

4. Barbara Kantrowitz, "An Interactive Life," *Newsweek*, May 31, 1993, 42–44.

5. Quoted in David F. Noble, *The Religion of Technology: The Divinity of Man and the Spirit of Invention* (New York: Penguin Books, 1999), 17.

6. Colin Cherry, *On Human Communication* (Cambridge, MA: MIT Press, 1977), 112; quoted in P. Kim and H. Sawhney, "A Machine-Like New Medium: Theoretical Examination of Interactive TV," *Media, Culture & Society* 24, no. 2 (2002): 221.

7. Cherry, *On Human Communication*, 112; quoted in Kim and Sawhney, "Machine-Like New Medium," 221.

8. Stephen W. Littlejohn, *Theories of Human Communication*, 3rd ed. (Belmont, CA: Wadsworth, 1989), 175.

9. Brenda Laurel, *Computers as Theater* (Reading, MA: Addison-Wesley, 1993), 112.

10. Andy Cameron, "Dissimulations: Illusions of Interactivity," *Millennium Film Journal*, no. 28 (Spring 1995), http://mfj-online.org/journalPages/MFJ28/Dissimulations.html.

11. Chris Crawford, *Understanding Interactivity* (San Francisco: No Starch Press, 2002), 6.

12. Katie Salen and Eric Zimmerman, *Rules of Play* (Cambridge, MA: MIT Press, 2004), 67.

13. http://www.gamespot.com/xbox/action/eragon/review.html.

14. http://www.gamespot.com/xbox/action/wwiicombatiwojima/review.html?sid=6155612.

15. Doug Church, "Formal Abstract Design Tools," *Gamasutra*, July 16, 1999, http://www.gamasutra.com.

16. Jesper Juul, "Computer Games and Digital Textuality" (paper presented at the Conference of IT, University of Copenhagen, March 1–2, 2001).

17. Salen and Zimmerman, *Rules of Play*, 64.

18. Steven Poole, *Trigger Happy: Video Games and the Entertainment Revolution* (New York: Arcade Publishing, 2002), 78–102.

19. Johan Huizinga, *Homo Ludens* (Boston: Beacon Press, 1955), 105.

20. Ibid., 46.

21. Rusel DeMaria and Johnny Lee Wilson, *High Score! The Illustrated History of Electronic Games* (New York: McGraw-Hill, 2002).

22. Mike McLaughlin, "Resident Saves Earth, Claims World Record," *Chapel Hill News*, November 10, 1982.

23. Bill Boldenweck, "Video Champ Blasts His Way into Record Book," *San Francisco Examiner*, September 6, 1982.

24. Charles Bernstein, "Play It Again, Pac-Man," *Postmodern Culture* 2, no. 1 (September 1991), http://pmc.iath.virginia.edu/text-only/issue.991/pop-cult.991.

25. Ibid.

26. Ibid.

27. Matt Barton and Bill Loguidice, "A History of Gaming Platforms: Atari 2660 Video Computer System / VCS," *Gamasutra*, http://www.gamasutra.com.

28. Georges Bataille, "The Notion of Expenditure," in *Visions of Excess* (Minneapolis: University of Minnesota Press, 2004), 117.

29. Ibid., 128–29.

30. Like Mario's coins, the cards could be converted into useful items, but anecdotal evidence suggests that most players chose not to use them that way, instead welcoming Triple Triad as a distraction.

Chapter 2: A Ballet of Thumbs

1. Hubert Dreyfus, "A Phenomenology of Skill Acquisition as the Basis for a Merleau-Pontian Non-representationalist Cognitive Science," 2001, http://socrates.berkeley.edu/~hdreyfus/pdf/MerleauPontySkillCogSci.pdf.

2. Maurice Merleau-Ponty, *Phenomenology of Perception* (London: Routledge & Kegan Paul, 1962).

3. Ibid., 136.

4. Dreyfus, "Phenomenology of Skill Acquisition," 1.

5. James J. Gibson, *The Ecological Approach to Visual Perception* (Hillside, NJ: Lawrence Erlbaum, 1986).

6. Ibid.

7. Merleau-Ponty, *Phenomenology of Perception*, 146.

8. Ibid., 153.

9. Hubert Dreyfus, "The Current Relevance of Merleau-Ponty's Phenomenology of Embodiment," *The Electronic Journal of Analytic Philosophy* 4 (Spring 1996), http://ejap.louisiana.edu/EJAP/1996.spring/dreyfus.1996.spring.html

10. Ibid.

11. David Sudnow, *Ways of the Hand: A Rewritten Account* (Cambridge, MA: MIT Press, 2001), 12.

12. Dreyfus, "Current Relevance of Merleau-Ponty's Phenomenology of Embodiment."

13. Ibid.

14. Poole, *Trigger Happy*, 182.

15. Andrew Burn, David Buckingham, Diane Carr, and Gareth Schott, *Computer Games: Text, Narrative, and Play* (Cambridge, UK: Polity Press, 2006), 56.

16. George Herbert Mead, *Mind, Self, and Society: From the Standpoint of a Social Behaviorist* (Chicago: University of Chicago Press, 1967).

17. See Donald Horton and R. Richard Wohl, "Mass Communication and Para-social Interaction: Observations on Intimacy at a Distance," *Psychiatry* 19 (1956): 215–29; also Donald Horton and Anselm Strauss, "Interaction in Audience Participation Shows," *American Journal of Sociology* 62 (1957): 579–87.

18. G. J. Ellis, S. K. Streeter, and J. D. Engelbrecht, "Television Characters as Significant Others and the Process of Vicarious Role Taking," *Journal of Family Issues* 4 (1983): 367–84.

19. Byron Reeves and Clifford Nass, *The Media Equation: How People Treat Computers, Television, and New Media Like Real People and Places* (Stanford, CA: Center for the Study of Language and Information, 1996).

20. For example, Daniel McDonald and Hyeok Kim, "When I Die, I Feel Small: Electronic Game Characters and the Social Self," *Journal of Broadcasting and Electronic Media* 45, no. 2 (2001): 241–58.

21. Gary Selnow, "The Fall and Rise of Video Games," *Journal of Popular Culture* 21, no. 1 (Summer 1987): 58.

22. McDonald and Kim, "When I Die, I Feel Small," 250.

23. James Paul Gee, *What Video Games Have to Teach Us about Learning and Literacy* (Hampshire, England: Palgrave Macmillan, 2004), 51–73.

24. Ibid., 54.

25. Ibid., 55.

26. Ibid.

27. Ibid.

28. Sherry Turkle, "Who Am We?" *Wired* 4, no. 1 (January 1996), http://www.wired.com.

29. Jeppe Bo Pedersen, "Are Professional Gamers Different? Survey on Online Gaming," *Game Research*, May 16, 2006, http://game-research.com.

30. Dreyfus, "Current Relevance of Merleau-Ponty's Phenomenology of Embodiment."

31. Aron Gurwitsch, *Human Encounters in the Social World*, trans. Fred Kersten (Pittsburgh, PA: Duquesne University Press, 1979), 67.

32. Merleau-Ponty, *Phenomenology of Perception*, 139.

33. Quoted in Dreyfus, "Current Relevance of Merleau-Ponty's Phenomenology of Embodiment."

34. David Sudnow, *Pilgrim in the Microworld* (New York: Warner Books, 1983), 40.

35. Ibid., 45.

36. Ibid., 47.

37. Ibid., 48.

38. H. L. Chiesi, G. J. Spilich, and J. P. Voss, "Acquisition of Domain-Related Information in Relation to High and Low Domain Knowledge," *Journal of Verbal Learning and Verbal Behavior* 18 (1979): 275–90.

39. F. Allard and N. Burnett, "Skill in Sport," *Canadian Journal of Psychology* 39 (1985): 294–312.

40. S. E. Dreyfus and H. C. Dreyfus, "The Scope, Limits, and Training Implications of Three Models of Pilot Emergency Response Behavior," ORC 79-2 (AFOSR-78-3594), Bolling AFB, Washington, DC, United States Air Force, Air Force Office of Scientific Research, 1979.

41. B. Calderwood, G. A. Klein, and B. W. Crandall, "Time Pressure, Skill, and Move Quality in Chess," *American Journal of Psychology* 101 (1988): 482.

42. H. L. Dreyfus and S. E. Dreyfus, *Mind over Machine: The Power of Human*

Intuition and Expertise in the Era of the Computer (New York: Free Press, 1986).

43. Maurice Bloch, *Prey into Hunter: The Politics of Religious Experience* (Cambridge: Cambridge University Press, 1992), 3.

44. Ibid., 4.

45. Ibid., 5.

46. Auguste Comte, "Système de Politique Positive," in Gertrude Lenzer, *Auguste Comte and Positivism: The Essential Writings* (New York: Harper and Row, 1975), pp. 452-466. Quoted in David F. Noble, *The Religion of Technology: The Divinity of Man and the Spirit of Invention* (New York: Penguin, 1999), 85.

47. John Durham Peters, *Speaking into Air: A History of the Idea of Communication* (Chicago: University of Chicago Press, 1999), 179.

48. Ibid., 5.

49. Ibid., 139.

50. Ibid., 160.

51. Bloch, *Prey into Hunter*, 5.

Chapter 3: The Sweet Cheat

1. "Hacking Away & Rumbles," *Your Spectrum*, no. 8, October 1984, http://www.users.globalnet.co.uk/~jg27paw4/yr08/yr08_05.htm.

2. Ibid.

3. "Join the Jetset," *Your Spectrum*, no. 4, June 1984, http://www.users.global net.co.uk/~jg27paw4/yr04/yr04_60.htm.

4. The Jet Set Willy FAQ, http://www.mdfsnet.f9.co.uk/Software/JSW/Docs/faq/remakes.htm.

5. Ibid.

6. Ibid.

7. On a personal note, Software Projects' publishing of the POKEs piqued my curiosity regarding BASIC; wondering if there were any additional manipulations I could benefit from by changing the game's code, I spent months teaching myself BASIC, inserting a number of largely insignificant but still entertaining changes to the game.

8. Anonymous, "Hardcore Retro-Speccy Cheating Code," *Gnomeslair*, March 2, 2006, http://gnomeslair.blogspot.com/2006/03/hardcore-retro-speccy-cheating-code.html.

9. Mia Consalvo, *Cheating: Gaining Advantage in Video Games* (Cambridge, MA: MIT Press, 2007).

10. Gary McGraw and Greg Hoglund, *Cheating Online Games* (Boston: Addison-Wesley, 2007), 4.

11. Ibid.
12. Ibid.
13. "The History of Crash," http://www.nonowt.com/magfold/crashfol/crasho1.html.
14. See http://www.nintendo.com/systemsclassic?type=nes.
15. See http://web.archive.org/web/19961105032729/galoob.com/Genietop.html.
16. *Lewis Galoob Toys v. Nintendo of America*, Nos. C-90-1440 FMS, C-90-1586 FMS (9th Cir. 1991).
17. The case was at the heart of two more recent lawsuits, the first involving ClearPlay, software that allows viewers to automatically skip offensive bits in DVD-format films, and the second involving SonicBlue, a TiVo-like DVR. The narrowly defined Family Entertainment and Copyright Act of 2005, however, neither repealed *Midway* nor reaffirmed *Galoob*, leaving the matter in legal limbo.
18. Consalvo, *Cheating*.
19. David Sheff, *Game Over: How Nintendo Conquered the World* (New York: Vintage, 1994), 460.
20. Salen and Zimmerman, *Rules of Play*, 60.
21. "Top Banana" review, *Amiga Power*, no. 11, March 1992.
22. Ibid.
23. Huizinga, *Homo Ludens*, 11.
24. Amit J. Patel, "Amit's Game Programming Information," http://theory.stanford.edu/~amitp/GameProgramming/AStarComparison.html#S1.
25. Thor Thorsen, "Confirmed: Sex Minigame in PS2 San Andreas," *GameSpot*, July 15, 2005, http://www.gamespot.com.
26. Wildenborg's statement is available at http://patrickw.gtagames.nl/.
27. http://www.romsteady.net/blog/2005/07/my-take-on-hot-coffee.html.
28. See http://en.wikipedia.org/wiki/List_of_best-selling_computer_and_video_games.
29. Raph Koster, *Theories of Fun for Game Design* (Scottsdale, AZ: Paraglyph Press, 2004), 112.
30 Interview with video game designer, August 10, 2006.
31. Ibid.
32. Friedrich Nietzsche, *The Birth of Tragedy* (New York: Penguin Books, 1993), 63.

Chapter 4: The God Machine

1. W. H. Auden, "The Christian Tragic Hero," *New York Times Book Review*, December 16, 1945, 1.

2. Ibid.

3. Aristotle, *Poetics*, trans. Malcolm Heath (New York: Penguin Books, 1997).

4. In this context, it is interesting to note that the aforementioned elements have not been present in video games from birth. Pac-Man, for example, or even the early Link and Mario, were terrifically uncomplicated heroes, and the players, eager to peruse the games' craftily designed worlds, ignored— or were perhaps even motivated by—their unjust suffering. For both Mario and Link, characteristics of tragic heroes began to appear a few install- ments into the franchise, in the mid-1990s, by which point such elements were common in video games.

5. Nancy Sherman, "Virtue and Hamartia," in *Essays on Aristotle's Poetics*, ed. A. O. Rorty (Princeton, NJ: Princeton University Press, 1992), 178.

6. I am thinking here primarily about the work of Andre Breton regarding repetition and compulsion.

7. Aristotle, *Physics*, ed. David Bostock, trans. Robin Waterfield (New York: Oxford University Press, 1999), 239.

8. Søren Kierkegaard, *Kierkegaard's Writings*, vol. 6, *Fear and Trembling / Rep- etition* (Princeton, NJ: Princeton University Press, 1983), 131.

9. Ibid.

10. Kathleen Hall Jamieson and Karlyn Kohrs Campbell, *The Interplay of Influ- ence: News, Advertising, Politics, and the Mass Media*, 5th ed. (Boston: Wad- sworth Publishing, 2000).

11. Jeremy S. Begbie, *Theology, Music, and Time* (Cambridge: Cambridge Uni- versity Press, 2000), 75.

12. Ibid.

13. Augustine, *Confessions*, 11.20.26.

14. Quoted in Begbie, *Theology*, 78.

15. Augustine, *Confessions*, 7.11.17.

16. For an instructive discussion of this point, see Stephen Mulhall, *Routledge Philosophy Guide to Heidegger*, 2nd ed. (London: Routledge, 2005), 39–40.

17. Ibid.

18. Martin Heidegger, *Being and Time*, trans. John Macquarrie and Edward Robinson (Oxford: Basil Blackwell, 1962), 89–90.

19. Ibid., 98.

20. Ibid., 116.

21. Mulhall, *Routledge Philosophy Guide to Heidegger*, 53.

22. Heidegger, *Being and Time*, 167.

23. Ibid., 164.

24. Ibid., 154.

25. Ibid., 157.

26. Martin Heidegger, "The Age of the World Picture," in *The Question*

Concerning Technology and Other Essays, trans. William Lovitt (New York: HarperCollins, 1977), 133–34.

27. Ibid., 134.

28. Samuel Weber, "Art, Aura, and Media in the Work of Walter Benjamin," in *Mass Mediauras: Form, Technics, Media* (Stanford, CA: Stanford University Press, 1996), 78.

29. Heidegger, "Age of the World Picture," 132.

30. Elihu Katz and Tamar Liebes, "The Export of Meaning: Cross-Cultural Readings of *Dallas*," in *The Audience Studies Reader*, ed. Will Brooker (London: Routledge, 2002), 289.

31. Quoted in Richard Wisser and Walter Rüdel, *Im Denken Unterwegs* (Südwestfunk: Neske-Produktion, 1975).

32. Quoted in Robert Metcalf, "Following the Words: Heidegger's Account of Religion as *Nachfolge*," *Journal for Cultural and Religious Theory* 10, no. 3 (Summer 2010): 96.

33. Ibid.

34. Ibid., 98.

35. B. R. Rees, ed., *The Letters of Pelagius and His Followers* (Rochester, NY: Boydell & Brewer, 1991), 36–37.

36. James Madison, *Federalist Paper* 51.

37. Kathleen Marie Higgins, *The Music of Our Lives* (Philadelphia: Temple University Press, 1991), 167; quoted in Begbie, *Theology*, 103.

38. Ibid.

Index